the life of love

LEOPOLD BERTSCHE, S.O.Cist.

Translated by FRANK ALBERT

the life of love

Meditations on the Love of God

THE NEWMAN PRESS • WESTMINSTER, MD.

1964

THE LIFE OF LOVE is a translation of *Leben aus der Liebe* by Leopold Bertsche, S.O.Cist., originally published by Verlag Butzon & Bercker, Kevelaer, West Germany, in 1960.

Imprimi potest: Idesbald Eicheler, S.O.Cist.
Abbot

Nihil Obstat: John F. Dede, S.S., M.A., J.C.D.
Censor Deputatus

Imprimatur: Lawrence J. Shehan, D.D.
Archbishop of Baltimore

May 15, 1963

fOREWORD

This book does not pretend to give a systematic treatment of the love of God. It merely offers some "pearls" of love that might draw the reader toward a closer personal relationship with God.

The expression "love of God," so often repeated throughout the following pages, always means *supernatural* love.

The paragraphs are separated by ornaments, for each deserves a lengthy meditation. Yet the deeper context linking all of them together should never be lost from sight. Only a total view can lend to each separate statement its unmistakable meaning.

May the Holy Spirit, the personified Love of the Father and the Son, light up in the heart of every reader the fire of divine Love.

PREFACE

The present work needs no commendation. It speaks for itself. If God is love, our existential destiny is something else than being thrown into nothingness; it consists in being called to love. If the precept of love is the main commandment, then we have only one task to achieve, to make this love a reality, besides which we need not seek for anything. If every man lived according to this calling, all problems would be solved. The inner restlessness and dissolution of modern man would be overcome and all the social and political problems of the world would be eliminated. War and turmoil would become impossible, and physical want would be reduced to a minimum. Even death would lose its terror, for it would be looked upon and thoroughly understood as the final entrance into Love everlasting. Unfortunately, we are far removed from such a mentality. That is why it is beneficial to have all of this proposed again and again to our spiritual understanding.

This is achieved here, not in the form of a scientific treatise, but by way of presenting maxims, mottoes, and statements borrowed from the saints and other giants of the spiritual life who, in fact, do nothing but elaborate on what the revealing Word of God had told us. It goes without saying that these sentences are not meant to be read one after the other in one sitting; they should be subject to careful consideration and thorough meditation. It is a wonderful thing that books such as this should be published today, for the frenzied pace of our times tends to make us "fly through" even our reading. What is truly essential always requires time and depth; and depth again calls for slow, patient immersion in one's own self. By its very method, therefore, the book makes for timely and wholesome reading.

May it help a great number of people to arrive at the depth of contemplation, the only fertile ground of that love to which the whole book is dedicated and which is the only enduring treasure in this fleeting world.

Thus any commendation could consist only in repeating the warning of the Apostle who concludes his hymn of love with these words: "Aim at charity!" (1 Cor. 13:14.)

DR. RUDOLF GRABER

contents

the life of love

the witness of holy scripture

1. Therefore, you shall love the Lord, your God, with all your heart, and with all your soul, and with all your strength (Dt. 6:5).

+

2. Those who love me I also love (Prv. 8:17).

+

3. I will draw them with the cords of bounty, with the bands of love (Os. 11:4).

+

4. He who loves father and mother more than me is not worthy of me (Mt. 10:37).

+

5. Having loved his own who were in the world, He loved them to the end (Jn. 13:1).

1

6. He who has my commandments and keeps them, he it is who loves me. But he who loves me will be loved by my Father, and I will love him and manifest myself to him (Jn. 14:21).

+

7. Because iniquity will abound, the charity of the many will grow cold (Mt. 24:12).

+

8. Abide in my love (Jn. 15:9).

+

9. The charity of God is poured forth in our hearts (Rom. 5:5).

+

10. For those who love God all things work together unto good (Rom. 8:28).

+

11. I am sure that neither death, nor life, nor angels, nor principalities, nor things present, nor things to come, nor powers, nor height, nor depth, nor any

other creature will be able to separate us from the love of God, which is in Christ Jesus our Lord (Rom. 8:38-39).

+

12. If I should speak with the tongues of men and of angels, but do not have charity, I have become as sounding brass or a tinkling cymbal. And if I have prophecy and know all mysteries and all knowledge, and if I have all faith so as to remove mountains, yet do not have charity, I am nothing. And if I distribute all my goods to feed the poor, and if I deliver my body to be burned, yet do not have charity, it profits me nothing (1 Cor. 13:1-3).

+

13. Aim at charity (1 Cor. 14:1).

+

14. If any man does not love the Lord Jesus Christ, let him be anathema (1 Cor. 16:22).

+

15. Walk in love, as Christ also loved us (Eph. 5:2).

+

16. May the Lord direct your hearts into the love of God (2 Thes. 3:5).

+

17. He who does not love abides in death (1 Jn. 3:14).

+

18. He who abides in love abides in God, and God in him (1 Jn. 4:16).

+

19. This is love, that we walk according to his [God's] commandments (2 Jn. 1:6).

+

20. Keep yourselves in the love of God (Jdt. 1:21).

+

21. It is more blessed to give than to receive (Acts 20:35).

22. To win your love, God came down from heaven. To win your love, He died upon the cross. To win your love, He established the Blessed Sacrament. Did He succeed in winning that love?

+

23. Do many of your desires remain unfulfilled? Do you find that nowhere on earth can you truly feel at home? Might not this very dissatisfaction serve God's design? Might it not be His way of prompting, urging you to seek your home in *Him*? That it is indeed. God's love for you is beyond description. Where else than in His arms could you feel more sheltered, more at home?

+

24. St. John says: "*God is Love*" (1 Jn. 4:16). In truth, He loves you from all eternity. He loved you long before

5

you were capable of returning His love. He says to each of us: "I have loved thee with an everlasting love, therefore have I drawn thee, taking pity on thee" (Jer. 31:3).

Out of love He created us.

Out of love He saved us through His Son.

Out of love He adopted us as His children.

Out of love He sanctified us through the Holy Spirit.

Out of love He warns us.

Out of love He punishes us.

Out of love He grants us forgiveness. (Roman Catechism)

Not only is God loving, but He is Love itself. That is why you have the tremendous privilege of knowing that He loves you. But you must not forget that love calls for love in return.

+

25. No truth is more certain than the fact that God is your Father and that

all the love implied in the idea of human fatherhood is a mere shadow of the infinite love of your Father in heaven. In this knowledge you find a treasure of beauty and comfort beyond words. It brightens your loneliness, makes every pain and trial that befalls you appear in a completely different light, gives you courage when you feel powerless. It makes you rely on God for the solution of all the puzzles you cannot understand alone. If only the knowledge that God is your Father were your guiding light in your living and dying! Truly, God shields you from many evils He never even permits you to notice. He blesses you and those you love. He overlooks your frailty. Briefly, He is your Father in fact as well as in name. Such knowledge is happiness itself. (Frederick William Faber)

+

26. Incredible as this may appear, God cares whether we love Him. There-

fore, He tries everything in order to win your love.

He invites you—through His promises.

He attracts you—through the prospect of your own advantage.

He urges you—through His benefits.

He moves you—through His requests, His persuasion.

He obliges you—through His commands.

He adjures you—through His threats.

Will all this be to no avail? Woe to you if it is, for nothing is worse than love rejected.

+

27. Because God loves you, He cares for you.

You are in His hands.

From all eternity He has known the smallest events of your life.

He disposed everything for your advantage.

God cares for you as if there were no
one else besides you.

He bestows upon you countless
favors.

Renew, then, your trust in the love of
God every day and repeat: "The Lord is
my Shepherd; I shall not want" (Ps.
22:1). Let your life's maxim be this: I
shall walk as He guides me.

+

28. The love God has for us in this
very moment is a matchless love, one
surpassing all created love, one beyond
the comprehension even of the blessed.
It is a love God Himself appears unable
to contain; a love whose inscrutable
depth puts our faith to the test; a love
everlasting, worthy of God in every respect and containing as their sum all of
His perfections. How many more things
this love means for me! Care or neglect,
sorrow or joy, failure or success, offense
or praise—should I not be utterly indifferent about what I encounter? God

loves me! One would almost cry out, "Now is the time to die!" (Frederick William Faber)

+

29. The fastest, most certain way to find an understanding heart—a gain for every man—is to seek it in God. He gave us His only begotten Son who in His human nature has a true heart sharing your joy and sorrow. (Cf. Jn. 3:16.) This heart beats for you. It is full of mercy and kindness. It is anxious to win you over.

Do you have a heart for God? In other words, do you answer the overflowing divine love with true love in return?

+

30. Christ's heart was wounded so that in the visible wound you might recognize the invisible wound of love. (St. Bonaventure)

+

31. Divine Love, present among us upon the altar, speaks only of love to us, wishes to fill us with love alone so that we might render Him the kind of love He expects from us: a strong love, never to be overpowered; a pure love, without selfishness; a long-suffering love, ready for every sacrifice in order to achieve conformity with God; a preferential love, self-effacing and without reserve, surrendering itself to the hand of God; an obedient love, passionately embracing His will. (St. Margaret Mary Alacoque)

+

32. The mystery of God's desire for our love should be a cause of constant joy during our pilgrimage through life. It lends a new aspect to everything. A feeling of security as a heavenly gift fills and envelops our soul. There is nothing else we need, nothing else at all. Everything the world could offer is worthless when compared with this yearning of

God for us. Our heart is full to over-flowing. There is no room left in it for more. The knowledge of God's desire for our love solves all of the problems of our inner life. It sooths our passing feelings of inadequacy while prompting us to strive for higher goals. (Frederick William Faber)

+

33. Love is the only reason why Jesus sometimes appears indifferent and cool toward you, for He wishes to lead you on the way toward a pure and unselfish love. Love is the only reason why He does not always act according to your will, for that might often be to your disadvantage and turn out to be a cause of unhappiness. Love is the only reason why He does not always answer your request, for He knows that the thing you desire would only harm your soul. Love is the only reason why He gives you this or that cross to bear, for He wishes to make you holy. Always, without excep-

tion, He is inspired by the love He has
for you.

+

34. The Bible is a revelation of love.
It is, however, not the only disclosure of
love. Each of us also receives a special,
entirely personal revelation of divine
love. We realize this when we consider
the fatherly providence watching over
our lives. Who can look back upon the
long chain of graces that make up his
entire life since Baptism without being
overcome by the wonder of this relentless guidance extending over every detail,
no matter how small? How often has
every one of us seen events take a happy
turn, obstacles crumble at the precise
moment when they appeared insuper-
able, and temptations become a cause
of enrichment? We realized then that a
seeming chastisement was really a pledge
of love. Every pain in our life had its
providential place. Missing it would
have meant a great loss. Having known

13

the people we chanced to know was important and advantageous. There are times when it appears to man that his whole past life is a masterpiece of the provident love of God. He did not, of course, feel this way at first. He did not always realize the extent of God's loving kindness, for what is more inconspicuous than the love of a father? (Frederick William Faber)

+

35. Nothing is more hateful in the eyes of God than sin. In His love, therefore, the Good Shepherd calls upon the sinner to mend his ways. He goes after him, knocks at the door of his heart, and follows him by His graces; He awakens in the soul powerful yearnings for Himself, and in fact lets man understand that in His kindness He is ready to take him back even when no one else cares about him any more.

If the sinner sincerely repents of his misdeeds, a wonderful thing happens:

God forgives him. With great love He bends down toward him again. He makes no recriminations. He holds nothing against him. No man, indeed, can match the generosity of God our Father practicing mercy and forgiveness. The sea has bounds, but His mercy is boundless. He does not, however, dispense you from the obligation of good will.

+

36. *The Crucified speaks:* See how immeasurably I love you. Can you doubt it in the least when you behold Me? Who else has ever shown to you a love comparable to mine? Look at Me. Here do I hang, between heaven and earth, nailed to the cross and suffering tortures no word can describe. My head is turned toward you with love. I stretch out my arms to embrace you. I let my heart be pierced that you might find refuge in it. My blood, my suffering, my death is for you. Yes, I love you more

15

than you could possibly understand. And you? . . .

Give your whole heart to me. Do I not have a right to it? Or am I asking too much of you? I am not asking for your offerings: I desire you. Would you deny my request? Am I not in this terrible state because I wish to conquer your heart? Who could be worthier and more deserving of your love than I, the Crucified? Do you not hear my pains and wounds crying out to you incessantly: Love Me from the depth of your heart? Shall I continue to occupy the last place, behind all the trivialities of the world? Oh, give Love its proper place! Love me as I have loved you!

+

37. There are many things in God that we find difficult to grasp, but the least understandable is the overabundance of His love. (Frederick William Faber)

38. When do you think you were chosen to receive the sacrament of Baptism? At the first instant of your conception? At the creation of the world? At the time the angels were made? No: You have been chosen from all eternity. But why has God selected precisely you? There is only one answer: Because He loved you. The foundations of love, most of all divine love, are beyond comprehension. One loves because he loves, and love itself remains inscrutable.

+

39. If we are in the state of grace, the love of God for us is boundless, superabundant. The relationship then existing between Him and us is nothing less than friendship, for sanctifying grace brings with it the intimacy of mutual love. Who can fully understand what it means to have God for a friend? This friend is always near you. He never disappoints you. He is never guided by

selfish goals. He has only one desire: your happiness.

+

Love's Concern for You:

40. Jesus—your Mediator in everything you ask.

Jesus—your Advocate with the Father.

Jesus—your Savior from all the miseries of sin.

Jesus—your Physician in every illness of the soul.

Jesus—your Good Shepherd in every anxiety.

Jesus—your Friend in every situation.

Jesus—your Help in every need.

Jesus—your Teacher in the art of perfection.

Jesus—your Judge after death.

Jesus—your All in eternal life.

Therefore: Place nothing above Jesus!

Have no other thought
than Jesus!

+

41. For your *sake* did Jesus consent
to be rejected by the Jews; betrayed by a
kiss; tied with bonds; slaughtered as an
innocent lamb; exposed in shame before
the eyes of Annas, Caiphas, Pilate, and
Herod; accused by false witnesses; tor-
tured by scourging and mockery; defiled
by spittle; crowned with thorns; struck
in the face; scourged with reeds; blind-
folded; stripped of His garments; fas-
tened to the cross with nails; lifted upon
the gibbet; reckoned among robbers;
made to drink gall and vinegar; and
pierced with a lance. (After St. Augustine) Many are those who say they love
you. But who among them would be
willing for your sake to take all this
upon himself? No one but Jesus. Will
you let His unmatched love be un-
requited?

+

42. The damned souls will say: If only God had not loved us so much, the pains of hell would not be so unbearable. But to have been loved to that extent: what a torture! (St. John Vianney)

+

43. Do not take anything for granted. Say instead in full awareness every time you receive a favor: This is another sign of God's love for me. Not being used to this practice, you might find it difficult at first, but if you persevere, it is certain to become a treasured habit. The surprises, the attention God showers upon you will then captivate your soul, and you will be consumed by love.

+

44. God loves me! He covets, demands my love in return; He vies for it, placing on it a higher value than I myself do. To think that this is true, unmistakably true! (Frederick William Faber)

20

45. Being so great, God loves the small; He bedecks the basest rock with flowers. Who is to mark the bounds of the love of God? Be then comforted; you are not forgotten either. (Anonymous)

+

46. How consuming must be the desire for your love that burns in the heart of God, since He deems this love so precious and important! (J. Schryvers, C.SS.R.)

+

47. Do not be mistaken: No man can escape responsibility when God loves him so much as to bear the cross for his sake. (H. Lacordaire, O.P.)

+

48. Come back!—But could I? Would God be bothered with me now? —Oh, yes. His love for you is beyond imagination. Come back! . . .

+

49. In substance God asks nothing from you but your love.

+

50. What can you give God that is not His own?—Only one thing: your love.

+

51. The Lord says to all of us: "Give me to drink" (Jn. 4:7) which means: "Give your love to me!"

+

52. Christ's words upon the cross, "I thirst," (Jn. 19:28) could be completed thus: I thirst for your love.

+

53. To follow the Gospel means to have love in your heart. (L. Sales, M.C.)

+

54. The Almighty finds His paradise in the heart of those who love Him. (L. Sales, M.C.)

+

55. Do not worry about the things of the world. Only one thing is necessary: to love God.

+

56. If God is truly love (and He is, for that is one of the most important teachings of the Gospel), then the conclusion is inescapable: Your religious life must begin with the love of God. Or we could say: You must begin with fighting self-love, carry on through fighting self-love, and reach the end while still fighting self-love.

+

57. Every man is loved to an infinite degree, but no man ever loves enough.

58. You will become what you love. If God is the one you love, you will be "God"; if you love the world, you will be worldly yourself. (Angelus Silesius)

+

59. As sure as death, the man who has no love for God will love an idol.

+

60. As a baptized person, you really have one task to achieve upon this earth: to love God. Anything else you have to do is nothing more than fuel for keeping the flame of love alive in your heart. Therefore, all your aspirations, your every thought and desire must center upon one object: Jesus. How quickly you would then become an entirely different being!

+

61. The heart of Jesus speaks to us of a boundless love. But He asks also that we give our whole love to Him.

+

62. When at the end of our life we come to Jesus, He will ask us only one question. "Where are your wounds?" Oh, unique, incomparable words! May they strike at your heart and remain unforgettable! For those words are the sparks that will most quickly enkindle in you the flame of love.

+

63. Mary also has a question to ask you. You would certainly wish to know what it is. But are you prepared to reorganize your life accordingly? Promise it now, firmly and honestly. For only then could her question have any purpose. Her words are these: "I love Jesus; do you also love Him?"

+

64. The whole life of a religious man in communion with God revolves around love as its center.

+

65. At the first Pentecost, why did

fiery tongues settle upon the Apostles? To indicate that the purpose of announcing the Gospel was to inflame hearts. (After St. Francis de Sales)

+

66. The only answer to love is love.

+

67. St. Francis de Sales once visited a family of relatives who had a five-year-old girl, his niece. With his habitual congeniality, the saint asked her: "What happened to your pretty doll?"—"Oh, I threw it in the fire," said the little girl. "But why?" the saint inquired, astounded. His niece then explained: "I showed her often how much I loved her, but she wouldn't give the slightest sign of appreciation." What would happen if Jesus also had to say of you: "I showered upon him (her) all my love, but he (she) never showed any appreciation"?

+

68. God says to you through all created beings: "I love you; give me your love in return."

+

69. Is it not true that you feel most prone to discouragement when your efforts remain unsuccessful? "There, I have failed again," you are prone to say, and at once a host of disheartening thoughts assail you. If your *will* lets these thoughts break in, great damage is done and gloom has won its first victory. Worse things will follow unless you stand up and fight the invasion. But how? you ask. First, make without delay an act of perfect sorrow. That should not take long. Then say to Jesus: "*Now I am ready to love you very much again.*" Apply this rule whenever you fail, whether it was a mere external blunder you committed, or a venial fault, or, God forbid, a serious sin. (In the latter case, however, you must also go to Confession before receiving the Blessed

27

Sacrament.) Doing this, you do the right thing. Discouragement would not have helped; rather, it would have made things worse. But now your state has truly improved. Sorrow out of love compensates at least in part for the fault committed. What is still wanting can be supplemented by a firm resolution that, precisely because you have failed, you intend to love God all the more. Every fault, every failure, every sin becomes thus an incentive for you to love Jesus all the more intimately. What a tremendous gain! We might even try to put it into figures: Your fault, let us say, caused you a five per cent loss; but the rise in love is a twenty per cent gain. Why then should you be sad?

+

70. Trouble, disappointment, and sorrow befall you. In their wake come the attacks of sadness and near-despair. You must make certain you do not surrender under any circumstances. But

how can you actually win the battle? One weapon that will ensure your victory is conversation with God. Tell Him quietly how much these hardships make you suffer. Just talking is bound to lighten your burden and renew your strength. Eventually, however, you must arrive at this understanding of love: Out of love for God you accept and bear the burden of the visitation. Sometimes another method will prove more effective: saying short prayers that, of course, must concern love. Whenever discouragement assails you, start saying an ejaculation slowly and with emphasis. Lower nature is bound to sigh under the pain, but you should not tire of repeating the prayer you have selected. This will ensure your final victory.

+

71. Have you been a great sinner in the past? If so, you have no choice but to make this resolution: Because I sinned so much, from now on my love

must be all the more consuming. In this way you not only make up for a sinful past, but you might even rise to perfect holiness.

+

72. Even if a man were cast into hell forever, it would be an immense comfort for him if he could say: "At least I once loved God on earth." (St. John Vianney)

+

73. The reason why many love Jesus so little is that few ever remember how *unspeakably much* He has suffered for them.

+

74. Can you remember when you were still a little first-grader? You saw adults reading big, thick books while you did not even know the alphabet. But were you therefore discouraged? Not in the least. Although it would seem that you had every reason to be dis-

heartened, in actual fact the thought of discouragement never even crossed your mind. If they have mastered knowledge, why should I not succeed as well? That in substance must have been your reaction—a healthy reaction, no doubt. The task you face today is to become a wholehearted Christian aflame with love. Do you think you should rather give up? Does the task appear to you impossible? But why should it? If so many others were able to reach the goal with God's assistance, why could you not also succeed? Do not fear. Keep struggling, fighting, and you will see that it can be done. You can be sure to get there if your "first love" is God. Keep at it, therefore.

+

75. Your "doing much" should amount to "loving much."

+

76. Talent, achievement, and success

31

count little; the important thing is to strive for "more" in love. (A. di Rocca)

+

77. You may not be able to spend a great deal of time in prayer every day, but you can love God. You are not able, perhaps, to go to daily Mass, but you can love God. You may not be able to fast as strictly as you wish you could, but you can love God. You may not be able to make a great voluntary sacrifice, but you can love God.—Should you become gravely ill, you can always bear the illness patiently out of love for God. Should you suffer contradiction, you can always offer it to God in a spirit of love. Should tiredness be your cross, it can be offered up as a sacrifice of love. And if you are overburdened with work, let that also be your offering to God out of love.—In other words, the greatest thing you can possibly do, loving God, is always feasible. If you are in the state of grace, there is no situation in which

you could not love God. Is this not the greatest, most comforting truth? Do therefore what you are expected to do: Love God about all else.

+

78. Wherever you happen to be, in the house or out in the back yard, in the office or on the street, you should "hear" this all-important question: Where is your heart? The question could also be phrased like this: Where do your thoughts wander? But that would not be the best phrasing. For as a rule your thoughts and plans, your imagination and dreams are centered upon the object that also occupies your heart, at least if we exclude the mental activity involved in doing your job.

This question saves you from being absorbed in the unimportant. It directs your glance to the one thing that is necessary. It keeps you from being overwhelmed by your work. It is a powerful motive for you always to walk before

God. It awakens your desire for a deeper love for Christ. All of these are advantages that ought not to be ignored as insignificant. Where, then, *is your heart?* Is it truly with God?

+

79. Every minute is passing, every hour and year; indeed, so is your whole life. But that is unimportant. The main thing is that you fill your time with the love of God.

Work, efforts, and trouble all come to an end. The main thing is that you offer them up in love.

Pain and suffering will come to you one day. The main thing is that you bear them patiently, out of love.

All your senses will eventually cease to function. The main thing is that you use them now in a spirit of love.

Your thoughts and words will be gone with the wind. The main thing is that they all come forth from love.

Your calling or profession will

eventually lose its importance. The main thing is that you now carry out your tasks in love. (After J. Koch, S.V.D.)

+

80. "I am truly a flame," say the last line of a poem by Friedrich Nietzsche, the prophet of the Antichrist. No one can quarrel with that statement. A flame he was, capable of setting afire and carrying away thousands upon thousands of souls. But Nietzsche was an *ignis fatuus*, not pointing to the heights but luring men into the abyss, the frightful depths of godlessness. Nevertheless, the same words sound as if they could have been written explicitly of you, a baptized, confirmed person. No motto, indeed, could fit you better than this: *I am truly a flame.* Be, then, the living fire of divine and brotherly love!

+

81. In your childhood you offered yourself up to God. You did not find it

hard to put your offering in words, to insist that you wished to belong to Him with every fiber of your being. But how much of an idealist are you now, knowing as you do the oppressive monotony of life day after day, knowing by personal experience how hard things can be, knowing how much it costs to remain absolutely faithful in all circumstances? Now is the time for you to translate your offer into living reality out of a personal, intimate love for Jesus. Remember always these words of the Holy Father: "Good and evil are engaged in a gigantic duel. No one today has the right to remain neutral" (Pius XI). No one, he says; and you are no exception.

+

82. In your mind and heart there should recur again and again this question of the divine Savior: "Do you love me more than these?" (Jn. 21:15)

+

83. Unhappy is the man who is satisfied with anything less than GOD and consumed by any other fire than His pure love. (St. Margaret Mary Alacoque)

+

84. Everything for Jesus! Anything that is not done for His sake is like letters written on sand. Do not be concerned whether or not men are grateful to you. Everything you do for Jesus' sake remains forever written in the Book of Life. However small the task that you are to do, do it with the greatest possible love. Say to Him and say to Him again those two little words that make every action holy: for You!

+

85. Everything with Jesus. Take these words literally. Perform all your actions together with Him. For He is truly in you through grace, and with a yearning heart He desires to do everything

with you. Let your slogan be: You and I, the two of us together!

+

86. Do you wish to rise to the heights of love? Free yourself, then, of the fear of falling.

+

87. Let Jesus be in your heart,
Eternity in your spirit,
The world under your feet,
The will of God in your actions,
And let the love of God shine
forth from you! (St. Catherine
of Genoa)

+

88. An act of love is never wasted, at any time, in any circumstances.

+

89. All of the saints desired to love the Lord more than He has ever been loved before. (L. Sales, M.C.)

+

90. It is all-important for our love of God that we esteem Him higher than

everything else in the world. Does our conduct in life prove that this is more for us than empty words? Would outsiders who see our daily life be compelled to admit that in all truth nothing is as important for us as God? Does our love for God unmistakably hold the first place before any other love in our heart? (Frederick William Faber)

+

91. Who among us can be fully certain that there was a single act in his life performed truly and solely out of love for God? But if this has so seldom—or never—been the case, that is no reason why it should continue to be so.

+

92. God Himself has implanted in us the capacity of loving Him. What He expects from us in return are deeds born of love.

+

93. Supernatural love should be the mainspring of all your actions.

94. Be anxious to inebriate yourself with the wine of divine love and drown in its mighty stream any other love you have. (Matthias Scheeben)

+

95. A hurdle is no real obstacle for love; it is rather a challenge. (M. Rosa)

+

96. If you would only refuse to strive for nothing, absolutely nothing else than loving God and bearing any pain with the greatest love imaginable! That is all you need for achieving inner perfection.

+

97. No man will be disappointed if he is daring enough to channel a lonely spring toward the Ocean of eternal Love.

+

98. Nothing is unimportant if it becomes an obstacle to love. (René Voillaume)

99. The man who loves God is concerned only with getting away from himself and letting his entire being be flooded with waves of divine love.

+

100. Love for the infinite Being claims everything you have, but it also contains the promise of every richness.

+

101. Let your faith in love never waver. Any suffering you are called upon to bear is only a sign that you are being loved even more than before. (Elizabeth of the Trinity)

+

102. Between you and God let love
   be the rule;
   Between you and the world, let
   it be watch and ward;
   Let hatred fill the gap between
   you and sin;
   And let hope be the bridge be-

tween you and heaven. (St. Mechtild)

+

103. Learning how to love God and our neighbor is our life's only assignment, the study of which will never be completed, for God does not wish that we set limits to this love. (René Voillaume)

+

104. Every man must strive with all his might to keep the fire of God's love burning upon the altar of his heart.

105. There is no end to love's rejoicing over what God is: God.

+

106. True love is concerned only with the honor of God. It has no time for the worthless.

+

107. Love's greatest pain is to see God offended.

+

108. The man who does not understand how absolutely empty all things are beside God has not yet arrived at the full understanding of the love of God.

+

109. Beware of any love that stops at words and is not expressed by deeds.

+

110. If you desire to win the friendship of Christ make sure that you never doubt His love.

111. Love is like a circle: endless. (Pseudo-Dionysius Aeropagite)

+

112. As God is infinite, our love for Him must be boundless. (St. Leo the Great)

+

113. Love always wishes to do what is more perfect, that is, what is more pleasing to God's majesty.

+

114. The Christian has reached the lowest rung of love's ladder when he no longer loves anything more than God, anything *despite* God, anything *like* God. (St. Thomas Aquinas)

+

115. Every true love is an act of worship, that is, an act that seeks self-annihilation so that the Beloved One might be everything and all.

+

116. Love thirsts for living presence.

+

117. Love consists in turning away from the creature and turning toward God, whereas the nature of sin is to turn away from God and embrace the creature.

+

118. The man who truly loves God is more glad over every honor given to God than over any honor bestowed upon himself. (C. Feckes)

+

119. The man who seeks himself has turned his back on love. (Thomas a Kempis)

+

120. The love of God consists in exchanging our being for that of God.

+

121. Love that does not trust is no longer love but fear. But fear that is

born of distrust does not honor, but rather wounds the heart of God. (L. Sales, M.C.)

+

122. Loving means emptying ourselves of all things that are other than God. (St. John of the Cross)

+

123. Having love and practicing it is better than knowing what love is.

+

124. The measure of love is not the amount of what we give but rather the force of our desire to give. (Fulton J. Sheen) Remember the poor widow's mite in the Gospel.

+

125. Who is nobler than God?
Who is greater than God?
Who is more powerful than God?
Who is richer than God?

Who is a more generous bene-
factor than God?

Who is more merciful than
God?

Who is more thankful than
God?

Do you see, then, why God is
worthy of all the love you can
give Him?

+

126. In the language of love, especially in that of the love for God, *I*
must be spelled with a small *i* and *YOU*
with capital letters.

+

127. Whenever we suffer, we always
feel and know it; we do not always feel
that we love. That makes suffering all
the harder to bear; but we always know
that we wish to love, and *desiring* to
love means loving. (Charles de Foucauld)

+

128. In loving we expend ourselves. (H. Roth, S.J.)

+

129. Loving means thinking not of ourselves but of the "YOU." That is why the man who loves will always ask: "What is YOUR wish?" (H. Roth, S.J.)

+

130. If you love the gift more than the Giver, your love is still imperfect. If you love the Giver more than you love His gifts, your love has reached perfection.

+

131. Love finds value only in that which is eternal and has no end.

+

132. To love and not to feel it is a real inner martyrdom. Not a few souls in such a state cease to practice the acts of love for fear that these acts would not

reflect the true feelings of their heart. But this is a mistaken belief. The heart may be cold and hard, but feelings are unimportant. What counts is the will to love. (L. Sales, M.C.)

133. There are men who cry because they do not love God. Theirs is the right attitude, for they are precisely the ones who love Him. (St. John Vianney)

+

134. True love is not concerned with being happy, but with *making* the object of its love happy.

+

135. Fear that we do not love God enough, qualm over loving Him too little, desire to love Him more and more: these are the unmistakable signs of our heart belonging to God. (Nicholas Grou, S.J.)

+

136. The God-loving soul is like an antenna receiving the messages of heaven.

+

137. Love is not satisfied with that

which is merely enough. Measure beyond measure is its goal; for if we are to
give everything we have, we must give
ever more and more.

+

138. Things sometimes stand still for
a while, but for love there is no standing
still. (Frederick William Faber)

+

139. Loving God because He desires
our love; loving Him because He loved
us first; loving Him because He loves us
beyond measure; finally, loving Him for
His own sake, for His boundless perfections—that, and that alone, is religion.
(Frederick William Faber)

+

140. The kind of love that founders
on the rocks of suffering is nothing but
self-love in disguise. (K. Bliekast)

+

141. When a loving heart has understood that it should ask for nothing but

God, it has understood everything. (F. Moschner)

+

142. We must love God *desperately*, that is, giving up all hope ever to love Him the way we really should. We must love Him with *fearless confidence*, that is, counting on grace but never counting the obstacles. We must love Him with a dynamic, reckfiless love, similar to a tree that sends its roots all the deeper into the earth as it rises higher toward the sky. (Frederick William Faber)

+

143. In their own eyes the lovers of God are the poorest of all creatures on earth, but in the eyes of God they are the richest. They believe they are far away from God while being as close to Him as can be. They feel as if they are forsaken by God while really being His dearest friends. They do not realize it, but their suffering stems only from the burning love for God that fills their

hearts. They may think they are the worst of men, but in actual fact they are the purest of all in the eyes of God. (From a medieval manuscript)

+

144. If you are uncertain whether you really love God, ask yourself whether you like to spend your time with Him in quiet and solitude.

+

145. Courage, lovers of God: Your love is most perfect precisely when you fear that you do not love. (A. Piny, O.P.)

+

146. It is in the nature of love not to seek its own self nor to retain anything for it, but to surrender everything to the beloved Person. (Elizabeth of the Trinity)

+

147. There is a burning desire alive

in every man who is filled with love for
God, for he who does not wish to love
God ever more intensely does not love
Him enough.

+

148. There is no shortage of pious
souls, but true lovers of God are rare.
(F. Mateo)

+

149. Love is never satisfied, for it
always wishes to give more, much more.
(H. Roth, S.J.)

+

150. If you do not dislike yourself,
you do not love God; if you dislike yourself a little, you love Him only a little;
but if you dislike yourself very much,
your love for God is really great.

+

151. Since love never believes it has
fulfilled all requirements, there is no
rest for love, ever.

+

Love's Way of the Cross:

152.   I. Love always accepts the will of God for its own.

II. Love finds no cross too heavy, no sacrifice too hard to bear.

III. Love conquers all obstacles.

IV. Love always finds a way to make others happy.

V. Love has no fear of men.

VI. Love is a guarantee of a royal reward for the smallest service.

VII. Love never complains.

VIII. Love is a source of consolation even amidst the throes of suffering.

IX. Love becomes more intense with every pain.

X. Love is ready to give up its very last possessions.

XI. Love bears the blows of

God's hammer with silent submission.

XII. Love is stronger than death.

XIII. Love keeps faith and trust when all else is driven to despair.

XIV. Love rests only in order to awaken to even greater love. (After Sister M. Berchmans)

value and importance of love

153. What makes a Christian great, really great, great by divine standards? Love. What is a most powerful magnet drawing upon him the good pleasure of God? Love. What gives his life meaning, substance, and depth? Love. What is his greatest help in trial? Love. What helps him overcome his faults triumphantly? Love. What can change him into a completely different person? Love. What enables him to seek nothing but God? Love. What bestows upon him immortal glory? Love. What makes him unwilling to exchange his present martyrdom for the delights of paradise? Love. What makes him cry out: Let God always be the Lord, even if I have to sacrifice my life for His reign? Love.

+

154. A good deed without the love of

God is similar to an electric light without power.

+

155. Cars cannot move without a motor. In like manner, our acts and abstentions are fruitless without love.

+

156. Love is the lifeblood of every baptized person, the principle of his basic attitude, the crown of all his virtues, the measure of his inwardness. (C. Feckes)

+

157. Love is worth more than long life on earth. (St. Thérèse of Lisieux)

+

158. Our deeds have all the greater value as they are accomplished with a greater love for God. (St. Francis de Sales)

+

159. Only a burning love for God can

break the bonds of selfish love, for love always leads away from the "I" toward the "YOU." Hence love alone holds the promise of success.

+

160. In entering eternity you will not have to give up your love. What is bound to pass away is that which lured you into spending false love on false idols. What is bound to pass away is that which kept you from loving God wholeheartedly and your neighbor as ourselves.—God and love are one and the same. God is everlasting. Therefore, love will also last forever, and so will all things born of love. (H. Kuhn)

+

161. Only love is important. Love alone can lend value to all else. Love is the only thing that counts by divine standards. When life is engulfed by the night of death, love alone remains aglow.

162. The smallest act of pure love is more beneficial for the Church than all other deeds together. (St. John of the Cross)

+

163. A soul is holy in the measure of its love for Jesus.

+

164. Only love can help us along the way toward our heavenly abode. The severity of self-denial is not the measure of merit; the love that inspires it is. What wins the crown for us is not patience in illness, silence in the face of slander, perseverance in prayer, or apostolic zeal and labor, but the underlying motive of love. That is the only decisive factor. The Lord looks at nothing but our love. He desires love, ever more love on our part. Should we, then, desire anything else than to love God, to love Him ever more? (Frederick William Faber)

+

165. It is a precious thing to love God; it is more precious to love Him ever more; and the most precious thing of all is to light up the fire of divine love in others. (Frederick William Faber)

+

166. Every sin is rooted in a deficiency of love.

+

167. In the hour of death we will find great comfort in being judged by the One whom we have loved above all things. (St. Teresa of Avila)

+

168. The most important act a soul in the state of grace can possibly perform upon this earth is that of the love of God. (Matthias Scheeben)

+

169. If it is true that the entire work of creation is nothing compared to divine love whereof all things were born, how much more true it is that all the works

a man can accomplish appear as nothing compared to a single act of love! (Matthias Scheeben)

+

170. The only kind of activity worthy of a child of God is divine love. (Matthias Scheeben)

+

171. The saints knew how to love: that and nothing else was their secret. (H. Lacordaire, O.P.)

+

172. Love is the only door that leads to the heart of God. (Blessed Eymard)

+

173. In the end everything depends on our love for God. (H. Roth, S.J.)

+

174. If all the riches granted to you through the love of God appeared before your eyes as they eventually will in eternity, you could not possibly close

your heart before this love. (After H. Roth, S.J.)

+

175. Without love for God there can be no fulfillment. (H. Roth, S.J.)

+

176. Holiness does not consist in knowing, seeing, and thinking a great deal. The great secret of holiness is to love very much. (St. Thomas Aquinas)

+

177. Love for God alone makes life really worth living. Without love everything is shallow and empty. This live relationship between "I" and "You" is indispensable. (H. Roth, S.J.)

+

178. Do you know what the capital sin of God's friends is? They do not love enough.

+

179. The deeper divine love pene-

trates the hidden recesses of our lives, until it becomes the soul and support of our every action, the more mature and rich life itself will become. (H. Roth, S.J.)

+

180. Nothing can compensate for a lack of love, whereas love makes up for everything else. (F. Mateo)

+

181. If you could only see who it is that asks you: Be mine! . . . Is it not time finally to open your eyes?

+

182. Happy is the soul that loves in truth. Through love the Lord Himself becomes the soul's prisoner. (Elizabeth of the Trinity)

+

183. What gives Holy Communion its value is basically nothing else than the love that fills our heart before, during, and after receiving. (F. Mateo)

184. Love for God is the remedy for all ills.

+

185. Nothing compares with the love of God whose effects are farther reaching than those of any other works. (B. Baur, O.S.B.)

+

186. How precious must be the love man is able to render if the infinite God condescends to desire it!

+

187. When the time has come for you to say good-by to life on earth forever, only then will you understand fully how right you were in letting yourself be carried away by the current of the love of God.

+

188. You remain vulnerable to all the things of this world as long as you do not learn the art of a perfect love for God. (Thomas Merton)

189. God has no use for souls that abound in knowledge but are devoid of love.

+

190. The devil fears only those whose love for God knows no limits.

+

191. Poor is the man who prefers to chase the vanities of the world instead of giving them up truly and vitally for the love of God. He has cheated himself out of what is the most precious and beautiful. (A. Rohracher)

+

192. Nothing more wonderful can be said of any man than this: he loves God with all his heart.

the effects of love

193. Longing for the treasures of this world dies in the heart of the man in whom the fire of divine love is aglow.

+

194. Zeal is an effect of love. The man who is not zealous does not love. (St. Augustine)

+

195. You like to receive mail from the person you care for, no matter how disagreeable the mailman happens to be who brings you the letter. In like manner, if you are attached to God through love, you will be glad to receive His message, be it joy or suffering. (F. Spirago)

+

196. Fire is never satisfied—nor is the love of God. (Scaramelli, S.J.)

+

197. Nothing gives more strength and comfort than love.

+

198. Where there is love, there is joy; where there is great love, there is great joy.

+

199. Look at the snow-covered yard behind the house. Can the snow last if all day long the warm rays of the sun keep beating down on it? No, the snow *is bound* to melt. In like manner, if your heart is filled with a deep, burning love for Jesus, your imperfections are *bound* to disappear, whatever their name and nature. As a God-loving soul you simply could not bear to offend Jesus willingly.

+

200. The man whose only ambition is to please the Lord will always seek that which is frugal, simple, and inconspicuous.

+

201. One thing is certain: When the powerful, holy love of God breaks into your life, it changes everything completely.

✝

202. Nothing creates closer bonds than love. Hence, everlasting life is a life in which loving and being loved will never end.

✝

203. The man who gives love its place will receive from God the abundance of every blessing in exchange. (C. Feckes)

✝

204. Love can never tire of praising the Beloved Person, God.

✝

205. A loving soul fears the God of majesty, admires the God of infinity, and is set afire by the God of love.

✝

206. Love means:
   Longing for God,
   Joy over God,
   Hope in God,
   Fear of God,
   Loyalty to God, and
   Gratitude toward God.

+

207. It is love's duty to eradicate everything of which Jesus disapproves.

+

208. Love is bold enough to go counter to worldly corruption, that is, to remain pure despite the surrounding smudge, truthful in a world of deceit and lies, gentle where cruelty is the rule, and faithful amidst all cowardliness. (After Terhofer)

+

209. Every God-loving man is a source of power, however inconspicuous, unknown, and plain the life he leads may be. (Frederick William Faber)

210. The man who walks on love's road need not worry about anything.

+

211. As a God-loving soul, show a glowing interest in becoming a saint; you will then find the way much easier than you anticipated.

+

212. Love's fire makes even the fire of purgatory bearable.

+

213. The saints live in the fretful excitement of love. (J. Rounault)

+

214. If a man did not love he would not be tormented by doubts about his love. (Henri Bremond)

+

215. The man who loves does all things without painful effort, or if he cannot do so, he loves the very effort and pain. (St. Bernadette)

216. God cannot possibly forsake a soul that seeks no one but Him. (L. Chardon, O.P.)

+

217. For a man who desires nothing but love the very things that beset his soul as obstacles to love become a source of merit.

+

218. Every authentic love we show God produces three unfailing effects:
- a. It glorifies the triune God;
- b. It works toward the salvation of immortal souls;
- c. It sanctifies the soul of the lover himself.

+

219. Divine love is like a robber: It takes away all earthly attachments from us, until our soul can say to the Savior, "I have no other desire than YOU." (Segneri)

+

72

220. "If a house catches fire," says St. Francis de Sales, "we throw everything out the window." That is, when a heart is set afire by the love of God, it is bound to seek to rid itself of all earthly things in order that it may cling to God alone. (St. Alphonsus)

+

221. The love of God lends strength to us for overcoming our petty sensitivity.

Love delivers us from our own selves.

Love is the foundation of constructive works.

+

222. Love brings heaven to this earth.

+

223. An object of our love always appears to us in glorious splendor. (M. Francis)

+

224. The torrents of everlasting love

will flood the soul of the man who, with a total love of his whole being, gives himself to God.

+

225. A God-loving man may not know what light is, yet beams of light will radiate from him in this life.

+

226. Other things may bring you close to God, but union with Him can be found only through love.

love and conformation

227. You love God only if you love His will; the measure of your love for Him is the measure of your love for His will.

+

228. After your death your neighbors will come and ask: What did he leave behind? The angels will also come, asking: What did he send ahead of him? (E. Gierl)—The latter question will not frighten you if in a spirit of true love you have made it your constant endeavor to live every moment of your life according to the will of God.

+

229. You must have often heard the beautiful phrase: "Paradise on earth." If there is any such thing at all, you may be certain that it is shared only by the man who in all situations worships the will of God.

230. This invocation in the Our Father, "Thy will be done on earth as it is in heaven," cancels your right to criticize anything the Almighty may visit upon you.

+

231. Say always and everywhere: Thy will be done; for this is the surest and quickest way to holiness.

+

232. For what purpose did God give you life? That you might become a saint. Therefore, do not linger; you have no time to waste. Whatever God desires, whenever, wherever, in whatever manner, and because He desires it: let these considerations be your guide that day after day sets a course for your life to follow. There has never been, is not, and will not be any other way toward holiness.

+

233. Do what God wishes you to do.

Beware of forgetting this rule, or all your efforts will be useless. For all things outside the will of God, praiseworthy as they may be in themselves, have for you no value whatsoever.

+

234. Remember: You are on this earth to do the will of God. If you fail to do so, you do not deserve to live.

+

235. Unless you strive for union with the will of God, holiness becomes a faraway, misty ideal beyond your reach.

+

236. Whatever God desires must be achieved *the* way He wishes it done. Take, therefore, the excellent resolution of performing all ordinary tasks exceptionally well. In this way the small chores of everyday life become for you a source of the greatest blessings.

+

237. Another thing is equally im-

portant: The will of God must be fulfilled at the time when He wishes it fulfilled. Whenever, therefore, this holy will knocks at your door, it must find you ready.

+

238. The where is equally important, for your place is where God wants you to be, and nowhere else.

+

239. Finally, you must fulfill the will of God because it is His will. Oh, how wonderful it would be if this were the only motive of all your actions! You would not then be far from perfection. But how often you still do things to win the honor, praise, or love of men! And what is even more common, how often you seek in your actions only your own satisfaction! This should not be so; indeed, even those things that you do according to the will of God, such as prayer, suffering, and work, you should

do precisely because *He* wishes you to do them. In this way you give glory to God, make the angels rejoice, and serve your own advantage.

+

240. Since the man who loves the Lord desires to be His likeness in every possible way, he must think as Jesus thinks, judge as Jesus judges, praise what Jesus praises, condemn what Jesus condemns, value what Jesus values, seek what Jesus seeks, and will what Jesus wills.

+

241. The word yes is a little, simple word; but if it is used to embrace the will of God, it acquires a tremendous imporance reaching beyond time and space into eternity.

+

242. Again and again, even in a single day, Jesus stands before you, waiting for your "yes." "Tell the truth! Keep silent!

Do not insist! Do not be so sensitive! Make that sacrifice! Do not refuse to do that act of charity! Do not be envious!" —Such may be His demands. You should waste no time in making up your mind. Let your heart and lips be ready with the answer: "Yes, unconditionally yes."

+

243. When are we Christ's own sheep who follow Him wherever He goes, whom He can count upon in every situation? Only if we say "yes" when the Good Shepherd expects our consent, and "no" when He wishes us to say "no."

+

244. For eight years a man had been praying to God to let him meet someone who would teach him the way of wisdom. One day, as he was about to enter the local church, he saw an old man, his shoes falling apart and his clothes hardly more than rags. He

greeted the beggar thus: "May God grant you a good morning." The poor man answered: "I have never had a bad morning." "Well, may God give you good luck." The answer was: "I never had bad luck." Our man tried again: "I wish you all the happiness in the world." "I have never been unhappy," replied the bedraggled creature. When he was finally asked to explain just what he meant, he said: "I have never had a bad morning. If I wake up hungry, I praise the Lord for it. Should I be cold, I thank the Lord. If I feel miserable and despised by men, again I give thanks to God. I never had bad luck, for whatever God gives me, be it good or bad, pleasant or bitter, I accept it from His hands as a precious gift. Again, I have never been unhappy, for I have my will united with the will of God: whatever He wishes I also wish." (Narrated by Tauler)—Would to God you did the same!

245. One phrase should be your guiding principle, one short sentence you cannot repeat to Jesus often enough: Your will and my will are one and the same.

+

246. Thy will be done! That is the motto that made all saints holy. (St. Alphonsus)

+

247. Remember: Conformity with the divine will is the best means of glorifying God.

Conformity to His will sanctifies your soul as nothing else could.

Conformity to His will is the surest way to immunity from disillusion.

If you walk on the path of conformity to His will, your faith will be the most alive of all, your hope the strongest, and your love the purest.

Conformity to His will cleanses your

soul better than any other way of spiritual life.

Conformity to His will enables you to remain constantly in the state of prayer.

Conformity to His will makes you capable of turning every cross to your best advantage.

Conformity to His will will be your greatest comfort in the hour of death.

Conformity to His will is the way of life that suits you best and to which God calls you. (A. Piny, O.P.)

+

248. How many gifts of grace have you lost throughout your life irreparably through discontent, grumbling, and criticism! You forgot that according to God's design precisely your bitter and unpleasing experiences were supposed to bring you closer to Him. And that would have been the case if, yes, *if* you had accepted them with loving patience. But as it was. . . . Christ's tearful meeting with

His Mother on the way to Calvary was only a blurred picture in your eyes. Or at least this spectacle did not prompt you to give your heart to them at once. All that is going to change now, is it not? From now on you will be ready to say with a loving heart always, everywhere, and in every situation: "Your good pleasure, O Lord, is the guiding star of my life."

+

249. We must embrace with love the particular situation in which we happen to be by the particular disposition of God. St. Catherine of Geneva understood this so well that whenever she was asked what her wish was, she invariably answered: "I always will that which happens to me."

+

250. Holy Scripture offers to us a perfect model of devotion in the person of the patient Job. Having sustained the greatest trials, he said: "The Lord gave,

the Lord has taken away; blessed be the name of the Lord" (Jb. 1:21) When finally he was covered with severe boils from the soles of his feet to the crown of his head, his wife said to him: "Are you still holding to your innocence? Curse God and die!" But Job said to her: "Are you going to speak as senseless women do? We accept good things from God; and should we not accept evil?" (Jb. 2:9 f.) Yes, it pertains to God to dispose, and to us to accept His dispositions.

+

251. A servant of God was in the habit of often reciting the alphabet. Then he would say to God: "You may now put the letters together as you will."

+

252. A well-respected priest in Rome was once subjected to a series of severe trials. He accepted them without protest and bore his misfortune with ex-

emplary patience. One day a fellow priest asked him what that wonderful secret was that enabled him to stay merry and relaxed despite everything. He answered: "In whatever situation or mood I find myself, I always look up to heaven first. I recall that my main ambition should be to get there some day. Then I turn my eyes to the earth and tell myself how little room I will occupy when I am buried in its womb. Finally I look around and remember all those thousands of people who are much more unfortunate than I. All this helps me to realize where the home of true happiness is, where all our worries shall end, and how little cause I have for complaining." (A. Scherer, O.S.B.) This practice could also help you to acquire the virtue of patient submission.

+

253. Pharisaic piousness is repelling, true piety attracts. But when is piety of the true kind, pleasing God and leading

to holiness? The question is not hard to answer. Suppose the pious man's plans are upset. He must submit to something that does not suit his wishes. Something inconvenient happens to him. What will be his attitude? Is he content, resigned, willing? If so, you may be certain that his piety is authentic. But if he is upset and dissatisfied, if he grumbles and criticizes, you may take it for granted that his devotion does not amount to much, even if he has the reputation of being a miracle worker. For only that man can be a perfect disciple of Christ who has learned to curb his own will and always keep an attitude of patient submission. —That is the standard you should apply to yourself.

+

254. On the first page of every catechism we find this question: What is the purpose of our life on earth? Whatever the exact words used in phrasing the answer, they amount to this: We are

upon this earth to do the will of God and thereby reach heaven. The second part could even be omitted, for the man who does the will of God will reach heaven infallibly. Let, then, these words penetrate your heart well and deep: We are on this earth to do the will of God. Can you sense the whole impact of this statement? It expresses nothing less than your most fundamental purpose and duty in life. Does your life really follow this path?

+

255. For one thing, no reminder could be too emphatic for you that you should often, even every day, partake in the sacrifice of the New Testament; but you will not profit thereby too much unless you are prepared to fulfill the will of God.—You often receive Holy Communion. But its spiritual fruits will be very moderate unless you are determined to do the will of God.—You are

used to meditation. But this practice will yield little advantage unless you have made up your mind to comply with the divine will.—You are, perhaps, devoted to frequent spiritual reading. But what good is reading, unless your ambition is always to do what God desires of you?— All religious services, all acts of devotion have only one purpose: to help you conform your will with the adorable will of the Lord.

+

256. A non-Catholic was dying in a city hospital where Catholic sisters are employed as nurses. His seven children had gathered in the room. As the end drew near, the oldest boy, about 14 years of age, took his youngest brother by the hand, stepped right up to his father's bed, and said with tears in his eyes: "Pray as our father taught us to pray when he was with us: Lord, Thy will be done!"—As a Christian who re-

ceived Confirmation, you would not want to be outdone, would you? Be, then, resigned, even if things do not always seem to go your way.

+

257. You protest again and again at the altar of God: "Lord, do unto me according to your will." You must be faithful to your own vows. Would Jesus not be disappointed in you if in a moment of crisis you started to count all the "ifs" and "buts"? We do not make promises to the living God only to go back on our word afterwards. You may, of course, have fears when you take your vow—that would only be natural. But you can quickly overcome your anxiety. Just remember that the Person into whose hands you deliver yourself is the best, the most loving Father of all. Where could you be more secure than in His hands?

+

258. If you wish to know where exactly you stand, examine first your basic attitude. What is it on final count that makes you do or not to do something? Do you, perhaps, invariably choose what is pleasing and turn away from the unpleasant? Do you identify your pleasure with the will of God, and consider anything that is contrary to your wishes as being contrary also to His will? Beware! For if you constantly seek that which meets your natural inclinations, while carefully avoiding everything you do not like, would that not amount to catering to your own selfish will? Your question, therefore, cannot and should not be this: Does this or that suit my wishes or is it opposed to them? It should rather be this: Is it or is it not the will of God? *That* will determine your choice. Whatever God wills, you do it, unpleasant as the task may appear; whatever God does not will, you abstain from it, no matter how much you would

like to do it. Then only can you truly say: I live for *God*.

+

259. The man who accepts the will of God with a ready heart accepts God Himself.

unselfish, pure love

260. Oh, how pure is the heart that seeks only Jesus, nothing but Jesus!

+

261. You always desired to live near to God. Your wish, however, can be fulfilled only if Jesus finds in you an unselfish, passionate desire to efface yourself in pure zeal for His honor.

+

262. In the eyes of God every action that is not performed with His good pleasure in view amounts to practically nothing. Intention, pure intention is the all-important factor.

+

263. Most of your waking hours are spent in working. In God's design your labor is supposed to be a powerful means of sanctification. It will be exactly that if you do not regard the performance of the duties of your state as a mere

"worldly activity." You should not be lost in it, and most of all, you should never separate work from prayer. Faithful performance of your duties is not everything. The most important element is still missing: activity and prayer must be inseparably bound together. With zeal and perseverance you must work at making their bond ever tighter and stronger. An important, although not the only help in this regard, will be the practice of pure intention, that is, doing everything out of love for God.

+

264. Whatever your undertaking, you should always call to Jesus: *I do this because I love you.* Be it prayer, work, an act of self-denial or charity, say: *Because I love you!* Be it sickness that befalls you, or pain, failure, trouble with your neighbor, bad weather, change of jobs, just say: *Out of love for you!* Be it eating, sleeping, or recreation that you are about to engage in, or anything else at

all, one element should never be missing: your intention to do it "out of love for God."

+

265. Pure intention, that is, the intention of doing everything out of love, is easy enough to conceive. But to maintain it really pure throughout is bound to cost you considerable effort, for you will have to renounce every self-satisfaction, every selfish advantage. Be careful, then, always to renew your pure intention, especially if you happen to satisfy some craving whereby supernatural intention is obscured or altogether forgotten. Be certain to recall your motto: "Out of love for Jesus!"

+

266. If you are, soul and body, dedicated to the practice of pure intention, that is, to doing everything out of love only, your everyday life will bear the stamp of the spirit of Christ more clearly than before, your work will acquire soul

and life, and God's blessings upon you
will be richer. Your motto, "Out of love
for you," will help you considerably in
the full understanding of these words of
the Book of books:

"He who is just, let him be just still;
And he who is holy, let him be hal-
lowed still." (Ap. 22:11)

+

267. The darker the night of suffering, the more radiant the life of pure
love that emerges from it. (Charles de
Foucauld)

+

268. Every grace bestowed upon the
soul by God, every trial He sends, every
sacrifice He requires of us has only one
purpose: to cleanse the soul more and
more and establish it in the state of pure
love.

+

269. That life is abundant in love
which desires nothing for itself but is
ready to give everything to God.

96

270. It is necessary in every respect that you bear your share of the vicissitudes of life, for otherwise you could never reach perfection. Foolish is, then, the question: Why this freezing cold, this void I feel, this numbness? Why is it that every so often I have to force myself to do anything? Why is it that nothing seems to attract me?—All this becomes truly meaningful if you accept it with the willing "yes" of love.

+

271. "Charity is not self-seeking" (1 Cor. 13:5). That is, according to St. Paul, the fundamental characteristic of true love. That is what distinguishes it from everything else that appears or pretends to be love, but in fact is nothing but selfishness. There is a little word you should never forget, a word of immense importance for your whole spiritual life; a word at the sound of which the heavens rejoice, the earth listens attentively, and hell begins to tremble.

That word is: *unselfishness*. This word must become your guiding star if you wish the words of Scripture to apply to you in all truth: "It is now no longer I who live, but Christ lives in me" (Gal. 2:20). Every step you take in this direction is a gain.

+

272. Often it appears impossible to say whether a man is heading toward perfection or is moving away from it. There is no such doubt for the soul that has become unselfish; it is certainly forging ahead instead of retreating, for the man who seeks nothing but God's honor and the salvation of souls loses himself in God and God will abide in him.

+

273. From time to time the Almighty provides for you theoretical instruction about the nature of unselfishness. The means may consist in a minor enlightenment, a good book, a lecture, or a ser-

mon. Such theory is by no means a secondary matter. For the deeper your knowledge of the beauty, value, and importance of unselfishness, the greater effect these ideas may have on your practical behavior. The good Lord, however, knows better than any man that theory is not enough. For this reason He keeps putting you in situations wherein you can learn how to become unselfish in actual fact. Think of the inner dryness you often have to bear, the hours when you find nothing to your liking and the smallest action takes laborious effort, the painful instances of misunderstanding when your best intentions are interpreted wrongly. . . . Occasionally, your life of prayer is also beset by the same troubles. How unbearably long half an hour of prayer may appear! How you suffer from your inability to accomplish anything!—What is the purpose of all this? Life as well as prayer must help you become unselfish. Similar situations put the authenticity of your love to the test; you must learn to count not upon yourself but Jesus, to seek not your own satisfaction but His glory, to persevere valiantly even though you do not seem to gain any advantage, to turn not to yourself but to God. Such lessons are necessary, for love is not self-seeking.

+

274. The more you give up yourself, the truer your love is. (L. Feuerbach)

+

275. The man who is under the spell of the love of God no longer belongs to himself.

+

276. True love for God and improper self-love cannot dwell in you in peaceful harmony. Either self-love will have to yield, or the love of God. In order that you may worship God only and stop adoring yourself as a sort of secondary idol, He sends you humiliations: lack of

appreciation, injustice, etc. Since these trials serve such an important purpose, they belong to the greatest gifts of grace you can receive in this life. How will you deal with them?—Unfortunately, the weeds of self-love are rooted so deeply in your being that you cannot eradicate them by your own efforts. You need God's help. His assistance comes disguised as humiliations He sends upon you. His only purpose is your sanctification. These hard trials are the clearest manifestations of His love for you. Accept them gladly through an act of the will, unless you wish to remain an egotist forever.

+

277. Let us imagine a statue in the art collection of a wealthy prince. If the statue could speak, we could have the following conversation with it:

"Why do you stand there in the corner?"

"Because my master put me here."

"But why are you so absolutely in-active?"

"Because all I am supposed to do is stand here."

"All right, but what do you gain by just standing there the way you do?"

"Oh, I am not here to gain any personal profit or advantage, but only to obey my master."

"But in that corner no one ever notices you, not even your owner."

"That is no concern of mine; I fulfill his wishes and that is all I care about."

"Would you not like to move about a little and thus be more useful to your master?"

"Not at all. I wish to be only what he expects me to be."

"In other words, you do not desire to be anything else than a rigid statue in a dusty corner?"

"That is correct, I desire nothing else. I am content to be here exactly as I am, for that is how the person to whom

I belong wishes me to be." (After St. Francis de Sales)

+

278. If a man accepts with a joyful consent the fact of his own nothingness, the triune God is glorified in him.

+

279. The more determined a soul is to deny itself every natural satisfaction, the stronger and more selfless is his love. (St. Thérèse of Lisieux)

+

the love of sacrifice

280. The cross Jesus carried to Mt. Calvary for our salvation was a heavy cross. It was heavy by its physical weight, which must have been from two to three hundred pounds. It was heavy because He was exhausted after a sleepless night and all the tortures followed by the scourging and the crowning with thorns. It was heavy because He had to walk uphill while carrying the burden of the martyr's tree. It was heavy because the worst of all sufferings, the terrible nails and the hanging for hours from the cross, still lay ahead of Him. Yet Jesus accepted the cross—out of love for you. Should it not therefore be your greatest concern in this world to greet your own cross with an "Ave, crux," that is, "Hail, Holy Cross," out of love for Him? This should be easier for you to do if you remember that with every cross the Crucified Himself appears to you.

281. The heart that loves Jesus also loves the cross. (St. Francis de Sales)

+

282. In the light from above every bitterness appears as a gift of divine love. Only in this light can you possibly find any value in suffering. The dart of the goad is thereby broken. If you know how to change your cross into a sacrifice of love for God, the heavens will rejoice over the glory you thus render to Him. Do you understand now how beneficial your troubles can be?

+

283. In the raging storm of trials sing always the song of love.

+

284. Your most important duty is, and will always be, to fashion your life after the love of God. This fundamental truth cannot be recalled often enough. For that is what makes even the heaviest and most oppressive burden bearable or

even easy to carry. But your whole being must be quickened by an intimate, sincere love, and your heart must be filled with it to overflowing. In this manner every sacrifice becomes for you a gift of love you offer as a matter of course, with a merry, willing heart, in a spirit of love. A strange thing will happen then: You cannot find enough occasions for sacrifice. An unquenchable thirst will come upon you. You were afraid of the cross before; now you long for it. Only love can bring about such transformation. Love, then! In this way you will acquire not only a manly heart but also the spirit of martyrdom.

+

285. The love in Jesus' heart was all sacrifice; how could your love be without suffering? He embraced the cross; how could you hope to avoid it? He bore pain and bitterness; how could you be without them? Such a love on your part would indeed be of the strangest kind.

286. You should never cease to sing the "Magnificat" in recognition of the tremendous privilege of being allowed to suffer. "What?" you might ask. "Am I supposed to be thankful for the cross when I am glad if I can bear it without revolt?"—If such is your mental attitude, you should not be surprised that you remain forever poor and wanting. If you could only understand how foolish your stand is! Try, I beg you, to correct your error. Cast away all discontent from your heart. Conform your will with that of God who visits suffering upon you. However much the lower nature may protest in you, tell Him with sincere conviction: "I thank you, O Lord, for the privilege of sharing your passion." Repeat this often, and *then* try to question the most efficient way of dealing with every want and trouble!

+

287. Is there a love that is not put to the test sooner or later? Does not Holy

Scripture say clearly and unmistakably: "In fire gold is tested, and worthy men in the crucible of humiliation"? (Sir. 2:5)

+

288. Jesus is pleased to hear your solemn promise: I shall not leave you alone in your suffering. But do you keep your word, always and without exception? Do you keep it in pain, want, and humiliation? Your promise, these wonderful words, should extend to every event, however hard or unpleasant, that you may encounter. Whether tiredness or bodily pain makes you suffer, whether you meet with contradiction or disillusion, whether loneliness tortures you or your inner life is dry and disconsolate, whether you are hurt by misunderstanding or willful uncharity—in all these circumstances you must preserve your loving patience while you thus speak to the Crucified: I shall not leave you alone in your suffering.

289. As the Savior reaches Mt. Calvary He is stripped of His garments. He lets it happen. He could have easily prevented this through His divine foresight had He wished to do so. But no: Jesus desires to lend you proof of His exceeding love. He keeps nothing for Himself, not even His garments.

The event is rich in implications; it is an example, a call. The motto of the tenth station of the Way of the Cross says in substance: *Give up everything!* Did you do so in the past? Did you offer up your most treasured, dearest possession? It goes without saying that only love is capable of such sacrifice. Merchants count and bargain, but lovers simply give themselves away.

There is nothing Jesus desires from you more than all the love of which your heart is capable, a love above everything, a total gift and abandonment of your life to Him. Giving up everything as He did was extremely painful. Judge yourself whether He has a right to demand of you everything that you have. But remember: He will not be satisfied until you have delivered all of yourself up to Him, for such is the law of *love*.

+

290. Holy Mass is nothing else than Christ's sacrifice of love upon Calvary. As such it makes absolute demands on you and requires of you a readiness for total love. The Offertory, Transubstantiation, and Communion must be in a way repeated in your personal life. The Offertory takes the form of total dedication to Jesus. Transubstantiation will mean the death of the old man and the birth of the new. Communion will consist in the depth of spiritual life as an expression of close union with the Redeemer.

+

291. True victory over self means tak-

ing advantage of all the occasions for practicing acts of love.

+

292. If love cannot totally expend itself in sacrifice, it believes not to have done everything in its power. (C. Feckes)

+

293. No one's love for God is purer than the love of the man who in his suffering thus speaks to Him: You are Bounty itself. (O. Zimmermann, S.J.)

+

294. The man who cannot suffer for his love does not love truly. Suffering is the touchstone of genuine love. (C. Feckes)

+

295. Thinking that love is possible without renouncing self-love can never be anything but illusion.

+

296. In all truth, life becomes worth living not when we seek all available comforts, but when our love is ready for every sacrifice.

+

297. In doing penance—which you cannot avoid in any event—your motivation should be love. Love will eliminate the inhibiting feeling that you are under the pressure of a "must" or "should." It will enable you to say these joyful, blessed words: "I offer my gift freely." Then you can really do penance, for love makes you strong enough to bear its burden.

+

298. However deeply a child is absorbed by a game, when he sees his mother arriving home after a trip he drops his toys and runs to greet her with a joyful kiss. Putting down his playthings is, no doubt, a sacrifice for him that he would otherwise hardly be will-

ing to make; but a greater love, that of his mother, makes the self-denial easy.—The lesson is clear: If your love for God is great enough you will not shrink from any penance.

+

299. What can make us embrace the cross with love?

The *desire* of conforming more and more to our Redeemer. The quickest way to have this desire fulfilled is to bear every suffering in a spirit of complete devotion to God.—The *will* to serve the glory of God, for there is no better means of implementing this will than loving patience in every sorrow. The man who can suffer "in Christ Jesus" deserves envy rather than pity.—The *truth* that the world is saved through suffering and that we are expected to continue Christ's work of redemption.— The *fact* that every suffering borne in a spirit of love makes love grow all the

113

more, and that the love of the cross is
the summit of Christian perfection.

+

Loving Gratitude in Suffering*

300. I feel so poor.
Thank you, O Jesus.
Oh, these pains!
Thank you, O Jesus.
People will think that I simply
do not want to work.
Thank you, O Jesus.
Such brutal temptations torture
me!
Thank you, O Jesus.
I cannot even go to Mass any
longer.
Thank you, O Jesus.
Slowly, drop by drop, my
strength dwindles away.
Thank you, O Jesus.

* You may wish to change the following litanies,
adapting the invocations to your particular needs.

114

Not feeling but *will* inspires this "Magnificat" that the angels carry jubilantly to the throne of God. The Lord sends them back to bring you a full, overflowing measure of grace.

+

301. Nothing ties us closer to the Sacred Heart of our Lord than the cross that is the precious pledge of His love for us. (St. Margaret Mary Alacoque)

+

302. An embrace of love divine is all the more intimate as it is more painful.

+

303. Inner suffering, when accepted in a spirit of *love*, is like a cleansing fire that little by little destroys in the soul everything of which Jesus disapproves. (St. Margaret Mary Alacoque)

+

304. True love gives up not only everything it has but also everything it *is*.

305. You ask in your inner desolation when Jesus is to return.—As soon as you yourself are gone! For He wishes to be the only Lord.

+

306. That love is purer which loves without enjoying the feeling of love. (A. Piny, O.P.)

+

307. Being allowed to suffer for God is by itself a tremendous reward. He who loves will understand what I am saying. (St. John of the Cross)

+

308. Only he can reach the supreme goal of love who is determined to sacrifice everything.

309. Are you immersed in inner suffering? Trust! Jesus in His love prefers to leave you in the darkness rather than letting some other light shine before you, a light that would not be He. (After St. Thérèse of Lisieux)

116

310. Should not the man who is privileged to quench his thirst with the joyful stream of divine love be willing to drink also the cup of suffering? (After B. Wild, O.E.S.A.)

+

311. The fact that Jesus willed to save us through His cross should change the mind of every man who thinks it possible to find love upon this earth without suffering. (H. Roth, S.J.)

+

312. No love is so great as not to be in need of further cleansing through pain.

313. Prayer means receiving from God and (lovingly) abandoning oneself to Him. (F. Moschner)

+

314. A man's love will be as his prayer is.

+

315. Who is a prayerful person? The man who loves God and knows that he is loved by Him. (F. Moschner)

+

316. The state of constant recollection, which sets in only where an intense love for God is present, presupposes that we place a great value on everything divine. If you are in the state of sanctifying grace, your soul is a dwelling place of the Blessed Trinity in whom there take place unceasingly the "divine processions": the Father begets the Son, and Father and Son together

spirate the Holy Spirit. But only the man who has fully understood that even a thousand worlds would be nothing when compared to God, only the man who thus has the correct idea of the infinite greatness of God and the nothingness of all earthly things, only that man will really understand how foolish and futile it is to seek anything else than God. He knows that the greatest of all treasures is not to be found without but within us. Since love has taught him to value this hidden treasure, he returns again and again to the depths of his own soul, there to meet with a heart full of love the three divine Guests. He is "recollected." Let that be your ideal, too.

+

317. The love of prayer is a touchstone that reveals how deep and strong the desire of the soul is to seek the good pleasure of God. (O. Zimmerman, S.J.)

+

318. Silent, simple loving is the best kind of prayer, for it makes the soul receptive to the soundless speech of the Holy Spirit. (C. Tilmann)

+

319. The man who does not keep his soul all day long in a state of inner love for God will lack also in his prayer the feeling of intimacy.

+

320. That prayer is the best which contains the most love.

+

321. A great love is in no need of words [when praying]. (Romano Guardini)

+

322. The more mature our prayer, the larger the place love occupies in it with an invincible spontaneity, until it finally becomes the only master. (H. Roth, S.J.)

323. O God! Do that I love you beyond measure. Do that I love you with my last breath. Let me die rather than letting me live even for a moment without loving you. My only desire is to be allowed to love you forever. Amen. (Prayer from 1848)

+

324. O Lord, clouds appear not only in the sky, they sometimes cover my whole inner life. Everything seems so dark and hopeless. But I shall never doubt your LOVE, for the clouds of sorrow, like those in the sky, will pass. Do with me as you please. Whatever befalls me, I shall remain faithful to you.

+

325. *Thus Speaks the Loving Soul:*
O Jesus!
Let your Spirit quicken my soul.
Let your heart set mine aflame.
Let your passion be my comfort.
Let your death shake my whole being.

121

Let your teaching penetrate my mind.
Let your grace be my guide.
Let your will be my law.
Let your light be my enlightenment.
Let your wisdom fill me.
Let your holiness shape my life.
Let your truthfulness enlighten me.
Let your patience be my strength.
Let your humility be my perfection.
Let your obedience be my teacher.
Let your bounty be my source of life.
Let your faithfulness fill me with grace.
Let your poverty be my treasure.
Let your mercy be my courage.
Let your peace prevail in me. Amen.

+

326. O Lord, you are and shall forever remain my only Love. I shall never
love a created being as much as I love
you, and most certainly I shall not love
it more than you. There should not remain a single fibre in my inner heart
that would belong to someone else than

you. For you I live, for you I shall die. Amen.

O Holy Spirit!

327. One of the mysteries of the rosary commemorates the sending of the Holy Spirit. You gave us new life in Baptism, you fortified us with the grace of Confirmation. Yet what a sorry spectacle my Christian life has become! My sins are countless. I am lukewarm and indifferent. I am worldly and superficial. I do things out of sheer, dull habit. Where is the penetrating glow and fire of your love? Where is the splendid will to work with all my strength for the coming of your Kingdom? Oh, how long is the way that I have yet to go! Only you can help me. Cleanse me of all that holds me back. Fill my void and satisfy my wants. Remove that which hurts my soul. Let others ask for earthly blessings: good health, success, long life, or whatever else it may be called; I shall ask only one

favor: the plenty of your gifts of grace, for the abundance of your love. For in that I shall find the fulfillment of all my dreams, hopes, and desires.

Come, Holy Spirit!

---+---

The Prayer upon Which Everything Depends

328. My God! My soul is shaken when I hear your words: "I have this against thee that thou hast left thy first love" (Ap. 2:4). Yes, my first love has died; self-love killed it. What remains is a lifeless grave. Could I have lost anything more valuable? Could even the loss of my life have been a greater misfortune? Now I understand that my only source of life is love, your love. I see it, feel it in myself, for the whole life I was leading in the past hardly deserves to be called life. I could not wholly belong to the world, and I refused to be wholly yours. Thus I led a double life that slowly but effectively was bound to destroy me.

How sadly I mourn now that first love which was destroyed by my being in love with myself!

O Lord! Is there a way for me to return to where I used to be? Or am I now condemned to miss forever your intimate friendship? I would be driven to despair if I were not allowed to hope that in this regard also the dead may rise from their grave. Raise, O Lord, what has died in me. Give me back that for the loss of which I alone am responsible: my first love.

+

329. Say often to God: I love you so much despite everything. His answer will always be: And I love you even more, much more.

+

Ejaculations

330. O divine fire that burns and never goes out, set my heart aflame that it may burn only for you.

125

331. Everything I do or suffer, let it be done or suffered out of love for you, O Jesus.

+

332. You are my greatest love, O Lord, and that you shall always remain.

+

333. O my God! How long still before the blessed hour arrives when you will be my All in all? (Thomas a Kempis)

+

334. Is it not true, O Lord, that you and I love each other more than can be expressed in words?

+

335. I love you, O Lord, and I love your holy will.

+

336. Prayer in the hour of death: I am leaving to meet the One who is my Light, Love, and Life. (Elizabeth of the Trinity)

126

337. O Mary, obtain for me, when the day comes, the grace of dying out of pure love for Jesus.

+

338. In inner desolation: I love you, O Jesus, just the same.—If you could only feel this love!

+

339. O Lord, you are all mine, and I am all yours.

340. In one of the last letters St. Gemma Galgani wrote we find three sentences that testify to her great love for Jesus. She states: "I no longer care for anyone else than Jesus." Can you say this of yourself? Have all idols disappeared from your life? Is He the only person to hold you in His bonds?—In a further passage St. Gemma speaks of her consuming desires. She cries out: "Heaven, where love will be our only occupation!" Should not this same cry rise also from your lips? In fact, should not these words, said of heaven, apply also to your heart?—The saint concludes her letter by saying: "Jesus must know that I can no longer live without Him." Is this also true for you? It certainly should be. *Love*, therefore, *love* ever more!

+

341. When you are wounded by the

love of God, nothing on this earth can satisfy you. Even if the Lord offered to you all the beauty of the earth, you would say to Him: Is this what you give me? Is this all? Why do you not give me yourself?

+

342. When we try to explain why a man is imperfect, we can usually find and quote a number of reasons. We would say: He is not filled with God, the love of God has not penetrated his soul. He is empty, void inside. He lacks a deeper religious spirit. What should he do? Not a few will offer this advice: He must fight his faults and practice the virtues opposed to his particular passions. That is certainly the right thing to do; it is even indispensable. But it is far from beng sufficient; it may result in superficial success but will not thoroughly heal the soul. What such a man would need more than anything else is an intensive *love* for Jesus that pene-

trates his heart, a love that captures all his interest, powers, and attention. That and only that can really help him.

+

343. The best thing anyone can wish for you is that your familiar relationship with God enables you to see and taste the glory of divine love. If that happens, no earthly thing can cast its spell upon you; it is bound to appear to you as shallow and empty and will have lost all its attraction. What could then compare even remotely with Eternal Beauty Himself? If you achieve through love what God expects from you, you will enjoy this Beauty without end.

+

344. Most people believe that happiness can be found only in love. Hundreds of thousands would volunteer to bear witness to this assumption, and we must agree with them. The fact is, however, that no matter how pure and noble an earthly love may be, there remains a

certain void it cannot fill; a portion of the heart it cannot satisfy. The reason is that we are created for GOD. Therefore only *divine* love can satisfy us fully. It is true that happiness is found only in love, but in that love which we bear to the infinitely lovable Being who is Love itself. Jesus is the person in whom you meet this ocean of endless love.—Is your relationship with Him truly one of love? If so, you have already discovered the most precious treasure of all. If not, do not give up until you win His heartfelt love. Once acquired, this love will sate all your desires and make you happy.

+

345. We can save the world only through love, a love so much aglow that it prompts our enemies to call us dreamers, fools, and fanatics. (Fulton J. Sheen)

+

346. Intensive, deep love for Jesus!

131

Who could praise this love highly enough? Devote to it all your strength, all your powers! Every day you should recall a hundred times or more these words of Christ: "Where thy treasure is, there also will thy heart be" (Mt. 6:21).

+

347. In the matter of divine love WILL is the decisive factor. That cannot be emphasized often enough. Yet is it possible to persist in love without feeling? Not very well. The feeling, the glow of love, although not absolutely indispensable, is of tremendous value and advantage. Its impassioned power furthers the cause of inner perfection.

+

348. If a man really sets his heart on a goal, he achieves it whatever the cost. Set, therefore, your heart on having your life filled with love for God.

+

349. The question of what the motive power is that quickens the heart of a confirmed person is easy to answer: Love.—What kind of love? A true, pure, deep love for Jesus.

+

350. Others may abound in power and knowledge more than you. It does not matter, as long as you and yours can truly say: We abound more in the love of Jesus.

+

351. Love does not count or weigh; it is bent only on giving, giving as much as it possibly can. You may call such love foolish. Love will not be disturbed, for it has understood that "the measure of God's love is loving Him without measure." (St. Augustine)

+

352. When is your love for Jesus such as it is supposed to be?—When others, were they able to observe your inner re-

lationship with Jesus, would spontaneously be able to say of you: "He must have lost his senses." He who has ears to hear, let him understand. For if that is the case, you have conquered the greatest obstacle, and *that* kind of love will be victorious over every want, humiliation, and suffering. You will recognize such love by its fruits.

+

353. When is your love for Jesus deep and intimate?—If you love Jesus deeply *you will often think of Him*. That comes about spontaneously, without notable effort. You simply feel compelled to direct your thoughts to Him again and again.—If you love Jesus deeply, *you will wish to be with Him all the time*. You visit Him often in the tabernacle of a church or of your own soul. You wish never to be separated from Him. The time you spend with Him always appears too short.—If you love Jesus deeply, *you will often tell Him about*

your *love.* You will never find it burdensome to tell Him how much you love Him. You will wish to express your feelings again and again, and find the greatest joy in doing so.—If you love Jesus deeply, *you will like to speak with Him.* Conversation with others will mean little to you, whereas talking to Him (in prayer) becomes all important. The time thus spent will sometimes appear to fly.—If you love Jesus deeply, *you will wish to show by deeds that your love is genuine.* Words will not suffice; you will insist on showing by facts that you really mean what you say.—If you love Jesus deeply, *you will not shrink from any sacrifice in* order to please Him. The heart of love is sacrifice. True love cannot and will not survive without suffering. Rather, it finds happiness precisely in being allowed to endure pain and hardship for the beloved Savior.

+

354. At your first Communion you

entered a holy pact with the Savior. From that time you were to walk with Him hand in hand through life, until you reached that everlasting union which has no end. Try, therefore, to carry out this simply worded program:

Hand in hand means:

Living together;
Being at each other's disposal;
Maintaining a union of minds;
Trusting each other.

+

355. Hand in hand means *living together*. There is no longer room for lonely travelers. Self-love must disappear. There must be an end to one's obsession with one's own person. Living together means that you must do all things with Jesus. He must be a partner to every prayer you address to the Father, to every work you perform, to every suffering you endure. Your whole life must be based not simply on following Him but on being united with Him. You

must often repeat to Him: *You will be my Partner* in this or that undertaking. The will, design, and wish of Christ will be the rule governing your every movement.

+

356. Hand in hand means: *being at each other's disposal.* There is no need to prove that you cannot do without Christ's help. In like manner, it is clear that He never ceases pouring into your soul the power of His grace and that He showers upon you countless blessings. But does Jesus need your help? Absolutely speaking, no. Nevertheless He wishes to be helped by you. He desires to use you as His instrument. Through your mouth He will announce today the wonderful works of God. He will use your hands to dispense His blessings. Your feet will carry Him in His untiring search for the lost sheep. He will always be at your disposal, but you also must be ready to help Him in a spirit of love.

357. Hand in hand means: *maintaining a union of minds*. In other words, it means to think and feel alike. What He praises, you cannot reject; what He rejects, you cannot praise. The commandment of love implies that you must become like unto Him more and more. The conversion of sinners is very important to Him; so it must be to you. He is concerned about the fate of pagans; so must you be. Holiness of life rates very highly with Him; so it must rate with you. He attaches great value to obedience; so must you. Worldly attitudes are anathema for Him; so they must be for you. In every domain the two of you must walk hand in hand with trustful understanding.

+

358. Hand in hand also means: *trusting each other*. Astonishing as it may appear, Jesus trusts you who are a weak and sinful creature. He renews His pledge of trust in you again and again in

various ways, most often in Holy Communion.—Thus you must in turn give yourself to Him with full confidence. The billowing waves of sorrow, the experience of your own weakness, or the knowledge of your many failures should not diminish your trust in Him. Tell Him that you suffer. Admit your weakness. Confess to Him your faults. That is the way of showing to Him the greatest possible confidence. In this manner the ties of love and friendship will not weaken; rather, they will become all the more intimate. No doubt, despite even a burning zeal (which is, of course, a valuable treasure), you remain the one who constantly fails in things of lesser importance. But if you do not hesitate to show Him your wounds, He will not cease to be your Good Samaritan. Trust for trust.

+

359. If you center all your attention on the task of deepening your love for

God, your pitiful crawling in spiritual life becomes at once a soaring flight.

+

360. Your own heart may sometimes appear to you as a jungle, engulfed by the climbing plants of evil desires and crawling with all kinds of hideous creatures, your passions. The qualms of conscience create an oppressive darkness. What should you do about it? Use pick and shovel, that is, seek out the roots of every single fault and try to plant the opposite virtues at the cost of relentless, hard labor? Yes, that is one way you could follow. But will it lead you to the goal? Would you not some day throw up your hands and abandon the thankless task? Would it not be easier to set the whole wilderness on fire—that is, to work at acquiring a deep personal love for Jesus? Set no limits to your love. Putting your trust in the grace of God, do everything in your power while you are upon this earth. You will be aston-

ished at the progress you can thus make
on the road of virtue.

+

Love and Confidence

361. Without reserve or worry,
    I put my fate in your hands, O
        Lord.
    You are my present, you are my
        day to come,
    You are the yesterday I con-
        quered.
    Do not ask what I would like or
        wish;
    In your mosaic I am but a tiny
        stone, and
    If you place me where I belong
        in Your design,
    Your loving hands will hold me
        ever after.

(Anonymous)

+

362. Even if you loved God as much

as the angels, you should still strive for loving Him more.

+

363. Searching for unending love is the greatest adventure; surrendering to divine love is the greatest love story; fusing one's being with the love of God is the greatest inner achievement.

+

364. An epitaph: He died consumed not so much by illness as by the love of God.

+

365. What do "things" matter when two beings live side by side in unspoiled harmony, loving each other beyond measure, and one of the partners is GOD! (A. de Geuser)

+

366. False, passing values should never again entrap your heart, for all your love belongs to Jesus. Earthly love should never again inflame your feelings,

for He is your only flame and fire. The passing days should never again be marked by careless indifference, for He is your one and only treasure.—Such relentless love for Jesus is the actual content of your entire life. If anyone deserves your wholehearted love, He does —in fact, He is the only one who does. For only His love is immortal, eternal, never to pass away. We *live to love* is as true as truth can be when it is applied to Jesus, but only when it is applied to Him.

+

367. Souls penetrated by a deep love for God are a bloodless altar wherefrom the frankincense of love rises aloft. (After St. Methodius)

+

368. "I have come to cast fire upon the earth, and what will I but that it be kindled?" (Lk. 12:49). These are the words of Jesus. The question is: Do you

143

share this fire? You will easily find the answer if you further ask yourself: What am I mostly interested in? What do I like to hear most? What holds the strongest attraction for me? Can you sincerely say to all these three questions that Jesus, nobody but Jesus, is the one who holds you in His bonds?

+

369. A great number of people are fascinated by the things of this earth. How is it possible that Jesus, the Holiest, most lovable, most beautiful object of attraction did not captivate your heart? Why does worldly pomp draw you under its spell so much easier than the divine Lover of your soul? You received the sacrament of Confirmation and you do not know the value of the love of God? You carry fire in your soul and you are not ablaze with it yourself? Every day you receive in overflowing measure the gifts of love and you remain cold and insensitive? Jesus is begging

for your heart and you close your ears to Him? He stands again before you at this very moment. Will you once again refuse His request? Do not turn Him away. No one has ever been sorry for surrendering all his being to Jesus; you also can only profit by total surrender. Endeavor with all your might to become one heart and one soul with Jesus.

+

370. You will never arrive at a state of intimate friendship with Jesus unless you wage a constant war on idle thoughts and words. (L. Sales, M.C.)

+

371. The marks of holiness begin to appear on our soul in the measure in which our heart is filled with passionate love for God. Love is a better defense against sin than fear. Our inner conversion is more thorough when accompanied by love because then it is so much easier to achieve. Such love draws

Jesus like a magnet, for its spirit stems from His. He cannot let Himself be surpassed in the matter of love and affection. Without such deep love there is no spiritual progress at all, for that is the source from which we derive all the typically Christian virtuous dispositions: love of suffering, silence in the face of unjust treatment, thirst for humiliation, and so forth. Moreover, love intensifies our distress over the sins we committed and gives rise to a feeling of true sorrow, which is more precious for the penitent soul than any other spiritual gift. (Frederick William Faber)

+

372. Mary encourages her children to reserve their most refined and tender, most intimate and intensive feelings solely for the Holy Spirit, His good pleasure and the inpouring of His love. (B. Wild, O.E.S.A.)

+

373. Be not satisfied with merely loving God; rather, strive for falling in love with Him to the core of your being. (Mary Ward)

+

374. If anyone opened your heart, he should be able to see the name of *Jesus* engraved thereupon.

+

375. God wishes your love to be exclusive and undivided.

+

376. Be determined to die rather than not to belong to God *completely*.

+

377. Love Jesus to the point of folly, and in six months you will make more progress in spiritual life than you otherwise would in twenty years.

+

378. The second request of the Our Father, "Thy Kingdom come," should be the expression of your deepest desire, your most fervent wish, your most burning love: Hunger and thirst for union with God.

+

379. Considering how close your ties are with Jesus, how could you limit your efforts to the absolute minimum? Is it

compatible with your condition that you should care only about avoiding mortal sin? Could indifference and sloth still reign in your inner world? No, no. Love should be the king—deep, tender, attentive, and fervent love.

+

380. Whatever your undertaking, if Jesus asked you: "Why do you do what you are doing?" you should be able to answer Him honestly: "Because I love you."

+

381. Our every wish and desire, every act of hope, fear, trust, and joy should be directed toward God. Such is the law of love.

+

382. Only a deep and active love can implement the spiritual motto: Better, rather than merely well. And yet that is the ideal the world itself expects you to reach. The world applies to the Chris-

tian person the strictest measure of perfection. Although it may itself be the seducer, it does not tolerate in the Christian the slightest contradiction of fault. Despite all its antipathy or even hostility, it wants to see in him the purest ideal of a God-loving life. It knows instinctively that only those souls can eventually earn for it the gifts of grace and salvation that completely "sold" themselves to God.—The world in its manifold corruption cannot afford to be without your zeal for virtue.

+

383. What is the most important asset you should acquire?

A powerful religious idea, accompanied with fiery enthusiasm, and boosted by fearless courage.

These three will ensure in your soul the victory of the grace of God.

+

384. Do you wish to be a perfect

Christian, one whose life is in complete accord with the Gospel? If you do, your life cannot be a succession of days spent in dull indifference. An ideal purpose coupled with an energetic will must animate your every action if you are to carry out your immense, God-given task, that of becoming a saint. Go forward courageously. Let love be your greatest object. Love knows no boundaries; it never says "enough." It always strives for more. Following its lead, you will fulfill the motto: All or nothing.

+

385. The soul will be consumed by (divine) love to the extent of its surrender. (St. Thérèse of Lisieux)

+

386. If you wish to be able to say sincerely: "I am wounded by love," you must be concerned with the so-called small things, for these are the fabric of your everyday life. Therefore, do not

dwell upon the past or the future, but live in the present fully, doing out of a motive of love and as perfectly as possible what you are expected to do in this moment.

+

387. Whose love is really generous?— The love of a man who has an ideal purpose that he pursues with all his might; a man who is equipped with an understanding of the lofty and the sacred and sees before him a duty that he carries out more and more faithfully; a man who has a goal that he is determined to reach; a man whose striving forward is more that of an eagle than of a mole; a man whose hands will not let go of the burning lantern of zeal; a man who is not afraid of the thorny hedge of obstacles; a man who resists like a solid rock the surging waves of trial; a man who knows the value of the precious stone of divine life and will not let it lose its spark; a man who is aware that

the noble dignity of a disciple called to serve the Lord of Hosts implies a tremendous obligation; a man who keeps in mind that his entire existence must be a "Gloria in excelsis Deo" and who therefore has set his whole life upon a straight course toward God; a man who not only quotes but also keeps the rule: "Spiritual life is all-important"; a man who bravely fights against his evil inclinations and does not shrink from want, self-denial, or humiliation; a man who, knowing that he was born for a higher goal, resists entanglement in the maze of earthly vanities and guards against infection by the spirit of the world; a man who is noble, unsparingly faithful, helpful, and patient.—That is the ideal your own love should follow.

+

388. Can the "Sursum corda" of generosity be based on a man's own strength, his special capabilities, exceptional talents? Is a generous soul as bold

and courageous as it is because it relies upon its own resources? God forbid, for such an unbridled self-confidence would certainly lead it to the abyss. The generous man knows that he is small and weak. If he still reaches for the stars, that is, desires to climb the mountain of perfection, he does so because he loves God. This love enables him to reach out daringly for everything that is His wish and will. This love alone is the root of his generosity.

+

389. The man who seeks nothing but God will never walk in darkness, however much gloom and poverty he sees in himself. (St. John of the Cross)

+

390. What shall I do, O Lord?—The answer: Let me do with you as is my will.

+

391. There is no total self-abandon-

ment without a total surrender of self-love.

+

392. What is the secret of happiness? "His will," instead of "My will."

+

393. If your love is prompt and fervent, you can say after the candle on the altar:
I am pure,
My light is bright,
My flame is glowing, and
In serving Christ I spend my substance.

+

394. What is it, O Lord, that you like
      most in this world?
      A heart that is glowing with love.
                        (G. Pustet)

+

395. The greatest of all revolutions will come about when all Christians de-

cide to pattern their life uncompromis-
ingly after the Gospel of love.

+

Self-Abandonment

396. Let me, O Lord, walk blindly on
the path
That you have traced.
I do not seek to understand your
guidance:
I am your child;
Wisdom's font and Father,
You are my Father too.
Your road may lead through
darkness,
But it will lead to you.

Let come what might, according
to your will,
I am prepared,
Even if you never quench my
thirst
While I'm alive.
You are the Lord of time,
The hour is yours;

Your everlasting "now"
Shall once be mine.

Make everything come true as
  you have planned
In your design.
If you, then, calmly call for sacri-
fice,
Lend me your help.
Let me forget completely
My tiny self,
And do that, dead to self-love,
I may live for you.

(Edith Stein)

+

397. How intense is the flame of a
burning candle? You could not keep
your finger over it for more than a few
seconds.—Now, how intense is your love
for your Savior? Can it match the
candle flame? Are you literally consumed
by your total surrender to Him? Are
your eyes turned toward Him day and
night? Are you as firmly devoted to Him

as a man can be? Does everything appear to you worthless when compared to Him?

Make certain that the candle that will one day be lighted at your deathbed can testify: "He (or she) too was a flame." If the witness is a true one, your life will go out like a candle: consumed by love, the love of the triune God. That should be your way of dying. Be, therefore, a flame!

+

398. Love (of God) defies all limits. It does not care what people will think or say. It spends no time in weighing what would be the practical thing to do. True self-abandonment calls for total surrender. If a man is not inspired by love to break the alabaster jar of his own smallness and pour out everything to the last drop, he will never understand what self-abandonment and surrender are.

Only small minds keep asking: To

what purpose is this waste? Only the cautious and moderate speak of exaggeration when they hear that a person can be so overwhelmed by love that he would spend hours and days in constant prayer. Earnest men who lead a life of penance because they cannot forget their own sinfulness and the sins of others are called eccentrics and cranks by the common Christian. Apostolic souls who spend their talents in spreading the Kingdom of God are ridiculed as fanatics by the majority. Philistines will never grasp the greatness of love. (R. Gutzwiller)—But you do understand this greatness, do you not?

+

The Properties of Love

399. Your love must be *untiring*, that is, never at rest until it reaches its supreme goal.

It must be *immaculate*, that is, free of selfish designs and the spirit of the world.

It must be *uncompromising*, that is, striving for complete union with God.

It must be *boundless*, that is, always susceptible to further growth.

It must be *consuming*, that is, attached to God with passionate intensity.

It must be *invincible*, that is, conquering all obstacles with its burning fire.

It must be *insatiable*, that is, longing for God more and more.

+

400. You have been chaffering with God long enough. You have been shunning long enough the sacred determination of going straightforwardly to your goal. Why all this quibbling? The days go by and you are getting older, but in spiritual life you remain an eternal midget. This cannot go on indefinitely. Only the daring can hope to win the prize. Put an end to this constant vacillation right now and once and for all. Look for the straight line that leads from the periphery to the center.

Love God and ask no questions, have no fear or worry, and make no reservations.

+

401. To win the first prize in a lottery you must be daring enough to risk a certain sum. Three or four dollars for a lottery ticket may seem a great deal. But what does this investment matter if you win a hundred thousand dollars? Yes, you might say, but how can I be sure that mine is the winning number? You cannot be sure, not in a lottery. But your investment for winning the prize of love involves no risks. You will have to pay the required price, the surrender of every self-love. But once you have paid, you cannot fail to obtain the coveted result. Why hesitate any longer? Arise and in this very hour shake off the bonds of half-heartedness. The grand prize of holiness is worth every sacrifice, and it can be yours.

+

402. Divine love claims all your resources: your heart with its every beat, your mind with its every thought, your senses with their every impression, your soul with its every power. Honor the claim, and the gifts of God to you will be boundless. (L. Sales, M.C.)

+

403. We must not be concerned only with avoiding sin and imperfections. We should direct our efforts toward an unwavering perseverance in love. (L. Sales, M.C.)

+

404. Only that man has reached the extreme limit of love who has given himself away to the last shred of his being. (Paul de Jaegher, S.J.)

+

405. Although a man may be far advanced on the road of sacrifice, if he shrinks from the final sacrifice of his heart because he intends to keep it in-

volved in a kind of mental "marriage" with some created being, he will never reap the divine fruits of the Holy Spirit. (B. Wild, O.E.S.A.)

+

406. Unless the idea of love for God becomes an overwhelming passion, it will never result in anything truly great. Love can triumph only if it becomes the dominating passion of our life. (Blessed Eymard)

+

407. Let no one say: Great love always means excess, immoderation. First of all, that is precisely what love should mean, at least the love of God, and you can wish for nothing better than this kind of love. But is it at all possible to love God excessively?

+

408. Your relationship with Jesus should mean this: He gives me every-

thing He has; I give Him everything I have.

+

409. You must be convinced beyond a doubt that everything that stands in the way of love must disappear.

+

410. God will give Himself to you as you give yourself to Him. (St. Teresa of Avila)

+

411. If there is anything that should dominate your whole life, it is the love of God.

+

412. Christians unwilling to surpass their mediocrity give little and receive little; good Christians give much and receive much in return; the really fervent love with all their heart and give everything they have. (L. Sales, M.C.) Your place should be among the latter.

+

413. You will never make a good sailor if you are afraid of the sea, or a flier if you are afraid to leave the ground and daringly rise into the air. In like manner, no one can arrive at perfect love if he is afraid of the height and depth of holiness. (After M. Raymond, O.C.S.O.)

+

414. To speak to you in all frankness, I do not worry about being surpassed in glory after we reach heaven. That is all right with me. But as far as love is concerned, I would never yield the first place to anyone.

+

415. We are allowed to love other beings besides God, but there should be not a single being that we would not love *in* God and *because* of God. (St. Francis de Sales)

+

416. Love is a treasure that we ac-

quire only if we give up everything in exchange for it. Therefore, God puts all the just souls to the test to see whom they love more: Him or some fleeting creature. (F. Spirago)

+

417. Do not fear. No trial will ever defeat you if you live a life of love.

+

418. If we wish to wage a campaign against the atrophy of religious life, we must bear, impressed at least upon our soul, the stigmata of Christ, that is, the insignia of His love. Otherwise people will not believe us. (After F. Trefzer)

love of god, love of our neighbor, and apostolic spirit

419. The love of God and that of our neighbor are like two wings of one bird, two tongues of flame rising from the same fire, two streams springing from one source; they are like twin sisters. "If you wish to know how much you love God, examine your soul to see how much you love your neighbor." (J. Pergmayr, S.J.)

+

420. As the moon could not be bright if there were no sun, so also the love of our neighbor is lifeless without the love of God.

+

421. A heart full of loving-kindness has a high value in the eyes of God.

A heart full of loving-kindness is a

treasure everyone expects to find in a disciple of Christ.

A heart full of loving-kindness is the place where the pearls of charitable thoughts are born.

A heart full of loving-kindness is a source of words and deeds of love.

A heart full of loving-kindness can defeat all the existing forms of egotism.

A heart full of loving-kindness lends to our life a richer substance.

A heart full of loving-kindness is capable of the greatest sacrifice.

How can you acquire a heart full of loving-kindness?—There is only one way: get closer to the heart of God. Therefore, put everything on one card, that is, think day and night of only one thing, to grow in the love of God. Let this be the idea that governs your life from morning to night. Allow yourself no rest until it conquers your mind completely.

+

422. True love for God is most of all a tremendous example that others are bound to follow sooner or later. Not only evil, but also good has a contagious power. The first reaction may be one of resentment and contradiction, for your conduct is interpreted as a protest against less ideal attitudes. But let that not disturb you. It happens with every pioneer achievement. At first, people ignore it. Next, they reject it violently. Finally, they are all for it. Starting a revolution in the pursuit of holiness, that is one responsibility that you can well afford to take. Its effects will be far reaching, and all of them will be fortunate.

+

423. The love of our neighbor grows upon the fertile ground of the love of God. (J. A. Hamm)

+

424. Do you wish to ascertain

whether you live in the state of grace, whether you enjoy the friendship of God, whether you are a real disciple of Christ, whether you live according to His spirit? Ask yourself if you love your neighbor, if you love him *for the sake of God*. The answer to the latter question will also be an infallible one to the former. (St. Augustine)

+

425. Rich is not the man who owns much but the one who gives a great deal. (B. Wohrmuller, O.S.B.)

+

426. The more intimate and stronger your love for God, the brighter its rays will be.

+

427. No one can practice brotherly love very long in all its purity unless he is solidly anchored in the love of God.

+

428. Our love must be very great if

we desire the (materially or spiritually) poor to forgive us the help we lend *them*. (St. Vincent de Paul)

+

429. Love is genuine if it perseveres despite a lack of love in return.

+

430. When you find a book that you like very much, you try to persuade others to buy it, for you wish to see it in as many hands as possible. In like manner, a lover of God will wish to see Him loved by the greatest number of people. (F. Spirago)

+

431. When every fibre of your heart is sworn to the service of God, the driving force of love will push you up to the front line in the battle for the salvation of souls. You will be safe from the danger of having to cry out with the man who said on his deathbed: "I cared only

171

for myself; I am certain to be condemned."

+

432. We may become preachers, speakers, writers, organizers, or everything imaginable *except apostles*, unless our hearts are burning with the fire of love for the Lord. (L. Sales, M.C.)

+

433. Real love is incompatible with a mentality lacking missionary zeal. (Frederick William Faber)

+

434. There is a shortage of saints, a shortage of apostles only because there is a shortage of persons loving God.

+

435. If the personal lives of apostles were as holy as their activity is zealous, they would revolutionize the world. (F. Mateo)

+

436. You must be a point wherein the rays of divine love are brought into focus to be then poured upon the souls of men. (J. Schryvers, C.SS.R.)

+

437. God is concerned not with the amount of works we do but with the amount of love that inspires our works.

+

438. Those men only will know the secret of a true apostolate who are volcanoes of love. (F. Mateo)

the way of love

This is the Way:

439. a. Beware of offending Jesus deliberately.
    b. Train yourself upon the endless field of small sacrifices.
    c. Feed in your heart the flame of desire for more and more love.
    d. Consider meditative prayer as most important.
    e. Be keenly aware of the love God showers upon you day after day.
    f. Obey the will of God faithfully.
    g. Renew often the inner acts of love.
    h. There should be no gift for which you beg more insistently than love.

+

440. The man who is burning with

the desire of love will soon be burning with love. (St. Francis de Sales)

+

441. Complete distrust in oneself and in everything besides God opens the fountain of inexhaustible love.

+

442. A time when you strive with all your might to become a soul filled with the intimate love of God can only be a time of grace.

+

443. All the dross of self-love must be ejected before you can become an acceptable burnt offering of divine love.

+

444. We learn to write by writing; we learn to love by loving.

+

445. Regular and frequent attendance at Holy Mass is the graduate school of divine love. (H. Roth, S.J.)

175

446. The more determined we are in expecting from God the gift of love and the more untiring in begging Him for it throughout our life on earth, the more certain we shall be to receive it. (H. Roth, S.J.)

447. Many are those who think that repentance inspired by love is not true love. They are wrong. This kind of love is as valuable as any other.

+

448. From first to last your soul should be filled with genuine repentance. Born as it is of love, such lasting sorrow for having offended God has countless benefits:

It intensifies our abhorrence of every sin,

makes a lukewarm attitude unthinkable,

dampens our love for the world,

breaks the chains of evil inclinations,

boosts our concern for the eternal,

nourishes in the soul the spirit of penance,

makes us tolerant toward the failing,

deepens in the soul the feeling of humility,

brings about a greater appreciation of grace,

leads to boundless gratitude toward God,

keeps the will alert for every possibility of improvement,

inspires recollection and silence,

deepens our distrust toward ourselves,

strengthens our trust in God, and

renders more intimate our compassion toward Christ the Sufferer.

(After Frederick William Faber)

+

449. How late you were in giving your love to God, and how much this love still leaves to be desired! Does this not warrant the deepest feeling of sorrow?

+

450. There is no more appropriate place for awakening in your soul the feeling of sorrow born of love than the garden where you kneel before the Savior whose precious blood, running down upon the ground, is being shed

for you as an appeasement for your sins.
Here you will soon understand that your
sorrow can never be too deep.

+

451. Our love for God is deepest
when we are shaken to the bottom of
our souls by the extent of suffering we
inflicted upon Him. (Frederick William
Faber)

+

frequently used sources

Bertsche, Leopold, O.C.S.O., *Directorium sponsae*, 4 vols., Kevelaer, West Germany, 1956–1959; 2 vols., Newman Press, Westminster, Maryland, 1958, 1960.

Faber, Frederick William, Cong. Orat., *Opera omnia*, 13 vols., London, 1899.

Francis de Sales, St., *Theotimus*.

Roth, Herbert, S.J. and Marga Muller, *Christusvereinigung in Glaube, Hoffnung und Liebe*, unpublished manuscript, Salzburg, 1953.

Sales, Lorenzo, M.C., *Jesus spricht zur Welt*, Freiburg, 1953.

Zimmerman, Otto, S.J., *Lehrbuch der Aszetik*, Freiburg, 1929.

Numbers refer to those of the paragraphs. L = love.

The Witness of Holy Scripture

Call for L.: 1. God reassures us: 2. God loves us first: 3. We must love Jesus above all: 4. Christ loves us to the end: 5. L. requires that we keep the Commandments: 6. A serious warning: 7. Jesus' request: 8. Gift of the Holy Spirit: 9. A great promise: 10. Nothing should separate us from the L. of Christ: 11. Without L. everything becomes worthless: 12. Striving for L.: 13. A frightening statement: 14. Walk in L.: 15. St. Paul's blessing: 16. Lack of L., a terrible state: 17. Blessings of enduring L.: 18. Guidepost of L.: 19. Warning: 20. A saying of the Savior: 21.

God's Love for Us

To win your L. . . .: 22. Our home is in God: 23. Proof of divine L.: 24. God, your Father: 25. God desires your L.: 26. Loving Providence of God: 27. God's unparalleled L.: 28. Sympathetic heart of God: 29. Christ's special revelation of L.: 30. Holy Mass, a ser-

A Call for Love

182

L.: 69. Fight against sadness: 70. He who sinned more, must love more: 71. A saying of the Curé of Ars: 72. Why Jesus receives so little love: 73. Courage to become a whole-hearted Christian: 74. What is required of you: 75. The important thing: 76. You can always love God: 77. The all-important question: 78. L. alone is important: 79. Be a flame: 80. Now is the time to translate your offer into living reality: 81. The Savior's question: 82. Unhappy is the man: 83. Everything for Jesus: 84. Everything with Jesus: 85. What to do: 86. A warning of St. Catherine: 87. Never wasted: 88. The desire of all the saints: 89. Does God hold the first place in your heart?: 90. Solely out of L. for God: 91. What God expects from us: 92. L. as a mainspring: 93. Call for L.: 94. Obstacles as help: 95. All you need: 96. No man will be disappointed in divine L.: 97. To keep very much in mind: 98. Getting away from one-self: 99. L. not only claims: 100. Faith in L.: 101. St. Mechtild's desire: 102. The only problem: 103. Keeping the fire of L. alive: 104.

The Nature of Love

Joy of a lover: 105. The only concern of L.: 106. L.'s greatest pain: 107. L. not yet under-

stood: 108. Suspicious L.: 109. Never doubt
L.: 110. Endless L.: 111. Boundless L.: 112.
Doing what is more perfect: 113. The lowest
level of L.: 114. L. is an act of worship: 115.
L.'s thirst: 116. In what L. consists: 117.
Fruits of L.: 118. Self-seeking, the enemy of
L.: 119. The best exchange: 120. L. must be
trusting: 121. An absolute requirement: 122.
Practicing L. is more important than knowing
what it is: 123. Measure of L.: 124. God
deserves all your L.: 125. I and You: 126.
Desiring to love means loving: 127. Expend-
ing ourselves: 128. L. thinks of the "You":
129. Imperfect and perfect L.: 130. Where L.
finds value: 131. L. without feeling: 132.

The Marks of Love

Who loves God: 133. L.'s object: 134.
Clear proof: 135. Like an antenna: 136.
"Enough" is not enough: 137. No rest: 138.
What is religion: 139. True L. is not ship-
wrecked by suffering: 140. Desiring only
God: 141. How great should be our L. for
God: 142. How the lovers of God appear in
their own eyes: 143. An infallible mark: 144.
The paradox of L.: 145. The nature of L.:
146. A burning desire: 147. A shortage: 148.
Genuine L.: 149. An interesting fact: 150.

There is no rest for L.: 151. L.'s way of the Cross: 152.

Value and Importance of Love

Incomparable value: 153. Good deeds without L.: 154. A comparison: 155. What L. is: 156. L. is worth more: 157. To remember: 158. Only a burning L. can achieve this: 159. What is to last forever: 160. Only L. is important: 161. What is most beneficial for the Church: 162. An infallible standard: 163. Only L. can help us along: 164. Precious, more precious, most precious: 165. Sin is the root: 166. Comfort in the hour of death: 167. The most important act: 168. Incomparable value of acts of L.: 169. The only thing worthy of a child of God: 170. The secret of the saints: 171. The only door: 172. To remember: 173. If . . .: 174. A true statement: 175. Holiness means loving much: 176. What makes life worth living: 177. A capital sin: 178. A correct statement: 179. A most important distinction: 180. If you could only see . . .: 181. Happiness through L.: 182. What gives Holy Communion its value: 183. Remedy of all ills: 184. Nothing compares with L.: 185. How precious L. must be: 186. Only at death . . .: 187. As long as your L. is not perfect: 188. Souls for which God has no use: 189. Whom does the devil fear: 190. Spurning the L. of God: 191. Nothing more wonderful: 192.

The Effects of Love

L. puts an end to longing for the world: 193. There is no L. without zeal: 194. Readiness to accept anything: 195. L. is like fire: 196. A teaching of experience: 197. L. means joy: 198. The power of intense L.: 199. A lover's only ambition: 200. L. changes your life completely: 201. Heaven: 202. He who gives L. its place: 203. Untiring L.: 204. The attitude of a loving soul before God: 205. The meaning of L.: 206. L.'s duty: 207. L. is bold: 208. A source of power: 209. No need to worry: 210. A glowing interest: 211. Comforting certainty: 212. How saints love: 213. The torment of L.: 214. St. Bernadette assures us: 215. Unthinkable: 216. Obstacles become a source of merit: 217. Threefold effect of L.: 218. Divine L. is like a robber: 219. If a house catches fire . . .: 220. Power of L.: 221. What L. can do: 222. How L. looks at its object: 223. A man who gives himself to God: 224. L. as a light: 225. A truth to remember: 226.

187

quirement of L.: 263. A prayer never to be omitted: 264. Maintaining purity of intention: 265. Blessings of pure intention: 266. The dark night of suffering—pure L.: 267. God's intention: 268. Life abounding in L.: 269. The "yes" of L. in vicissitudes: 270. Charity is not self-seeking: 271. Forging ahead securely: 272. Unselfishness in practice: 273. When is L. truer: 274. A necessary consequence: 275. Love of God and L. of self: 276. Conversation with a statue: 277. In whom is God glorified?: 278. When does L. become stronger?: 279.

The Love of Sacrifice

"Ave Crux": 280. L. of the Cross: 281. The benefits of trial: 282. Do not cease to love in trials: 283. True L. makes man ready for sacrifice: 284. The criterion of L.: 285. Give thanks for the privilege of suffering: 286. The test of L.: 287. Your promise to the Crucified: 288. A station on the way of the cross: 289. What is implied in Holy Mass: 290. Victory over the self: 291. What L. believes: 292. The purest praise: 293. When L. is of the true kind: 294. When L. is nothing but an illusion: 295. Life worth living: 296. Motive of penance: 297. When L. is overwhelming . . .: 298. Why embrace the cross lovingly?: 299. Litany of gratitude: 300. The strongest tie: 301. Suffering and L.: 302. The purpose of inner suffering: 303. What else L. is ready to offer: 304. When is Jesus to return: 305. A profound truth: 306. A tremendous reward: 307. The supreme goal of L.: 308. Why the darkness?: 309. To drink both cups: 310. Consider carefully: 311. L. is never too great: 312.

Love and Prayer

What prayer is: 313. An immutable law: 314. Who is a true worshipper?: 315. How to be recollected: 316. The touchstone: 317. The best kind of prayer: 318. Your prayer is like your daily life: 319. The best prayer: 320. Wordless prayer: 321. The more mature our prayer . . .: 322. Praying for L. beyond measure: 323. Prayer in hardships: 324. Thus speaks the loving soul: 325. A profession of L.: 326. Prayer to the Holy Spirit: 327. A decisive prayer: 328. Say often to God: 329.

Short prayer for burning L.: 330. For pure intention: 331. For exclusive L.: 332. Prayer of longing desire: 333. Prayer of intimate L.: 334. Conformity with the will of God: 335. Prayer in the hour of death: 336. Prayer to Mary: 337. Prayer in inner desolation: 338. Prayer of total self-abandonment: 339.

Love's Death and Intensity

Three remarks of St. Gemma Galgani: 340. When you are wounded by L.: 341. Thorough healing: 342. Familiar relationship with God: 343. Only divine L. can make us happy: 344. L. is our only salvation: 345. Deep L. for Jesus: 346. Without feeling you cannot persist in L. for long: 347. Setting your heart on loving God: 348. What quickens the heart of a confirmed person: 349. Greater abundance of L.: 350. L.'s daily bread is profusion: 351. Marks of intimate L.: 352. If you love Jesus deeply: 353. A simply worded program: 354. Hand in hand—living together: 355. Hand in hand—being at each other's disposal: 356. Hand in hand—maintaining a union of minds: 357. Hand in hand—trusting each other: 358. No more crawling in L.: 359. A better method: 360. L. and confidence: 361. Never enough: 362. A description of intimate L.: 363. An epitaph: 364. Praise of union with God: 365. L. is life's content: 366. The frankincense of L.: 367. Three questions: 368. A pressing call: 369. War on idle thoughts: 370. Marks of holiness: 371. Mary encourages us: 372. In L. with God: 373. If anyone opened your heart . . .: 374.

God wishes . . .: 375. Determination in L.:
376. L. makes for soaring progress: 377. The
second request of the Our Father: 378. L.
should be deep, tender, attentive: 379. Question and answer: 380. L. is the guide of all
our deeds: 381. Better, rather than merely
well: 382. Your greatest need: 383. All or
nothing: 384. Keep in mind: 385. To live in
the present fully: 386. Whose L. is truly
generous: 387. Source of generosity: 388. The
man who seeks nothing but God . . .: 389.
Jesus answers your question: 390. First, you
must surrender your self-love: 391. The secret
of happiness: 392. Thus speaks the candle:
393. Christ's answer: 394. The greatest
revolution: 395. A poem on self-abandonment: 396. Burning L.: 397. Courageous L.:
398. The properties of L.: 399. No more
quibbling: 400. Risk everything—win everything: 401. Everything without exception:
402. Avoidance of faults is not enough: 403.
The summit of L.: 404. Do not shrink from
the final step: 405. Passionate L.: 406. L. and
excess: 407. An understanding: 408. What
must disappear: 409. An exchange of gifts:
410. L. must dominate: 411. Common,
better, and best L.: 412. Who will never

arrive at perfect L.: 413. In all frankness: 414. What may be, what may not be: 415. L. is a treasure: 416. Do not fear: 417. We must bear the stigmata of Christ: 418.

Love of God, Love of Our Neigbor, and Apostolic Spirit

Twin sisters: 419. A comparison: 420. Heart full of loving kindness: 421. Contagious example: 422. The fertile ground of the love of God: 423. Love of our neighbor as a criterion of our love for God: 424. The truly rich man: 425. It could not be otherwise: 426. A necessary condition: 427. A remark of St. Vincent's: 428. When is L. genuine?: 429. A wish stemming from L.: 430. L. awakens our zeal for souls: 431. There is no apostolate without L.: 432. There can be no L. where there is no missionary zeal: 433. Why there is a shortage of apostles: 434. If apostles were more loving: 435. L. is a focus: 436. What souls are dearer to God: 437. A volcano of L.: 438.

The Way of Love

This is the way: 439. Results of burning desire: 440. The fountain of inexhaustible L.: 441. Time of grace: 442. What must be done first: 443. How do we learn L.?: 444. The graduate school of divine L.: 445. Trusting prayer for L.: 446.

Love and Repentance

Repentance inspired by L. is true L.: 447. The countless benefits of repentance born of L.: 448. Too little L. is enough motive for repentance: 449. The quickest way to awaken sorrow: 450. When is our L. for God the deepest?: 451.

A NOTE ON THE TYPE

IN WHICH THIS BOOK WAS SET

This book has been set in Electra, a type face created in 1935 by W. A. Dwiggins, the well-known Boston artist. This type falls within the "modern" family of type styles, but was drawn to avoid the extreme contrast between "thick and thin" elements that marks most "modern" type faces. The design is not based upon any traditional model, and is not an attempt to revive or to reconstruct any historic type. Since its birth, Electra has met with success because of its easy-to-read quality. This book was composed and printed by the York Composition Company, Inc., of York, Pa., and bound by Moore and Company of Baltimore, Md. The design and typography of this book are by Howard N. King.

THE LIFE OF LOVE

*Meditations
on the Love of God*

by
LEOPOLD BERTSCHE, S.O.CIST.

As a collection of selected texts from the Scriptures and the writings of the greatest saints and doctors of the spiritual life, THE LIFE OF LOVE needs no greater commendation. Since the precept of love of God is the first and greatest of the Commandments, then the primary goal of life is to fulfill that obligation. Unfortunately, most men are so far from recognizing this law in their daily lives that it is important and valuable to have this repeated over and over again—not in the form of scientific treatises on the love of God, but by presenting the wisdom

(continued on back flap)